Evergreen Leaves

Swami Amritageetananda Puri

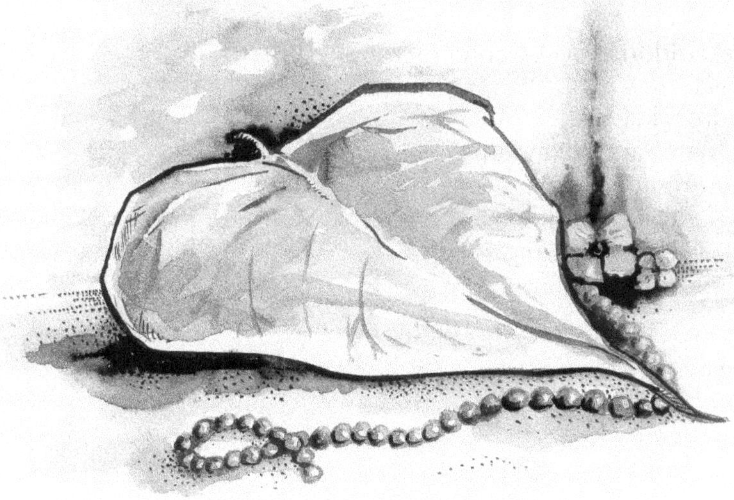

Evergreen Leaves
By Swami Amritageetananda Puri

Published by:
Mata Amritanandamayi Center
P.O. Box 613
San Ramon, CA 94583
United States
www.amma.org

Copyright © 2016 by Mata Amritanandamayi Mission Trust, Amritapuri, Kerala 690546, India
All rights reserved.
No part of this publication may be stored in a retrieval system, transmitted, reproduced, transcribed or translated into any language in any form by any publisher.

First Edition by MA Center October 2016

Address in India:
Mata Amritanandamayi Mission Trust
Amritapuri, Kollam Dt.
Kerala 690546, India
www.amritapuri.org
inform@amritapuri.org

Evergreen Leaves

Swami Amritageetananda Puri

Mata Amritanandamayi Center, San Ramon
California, United States

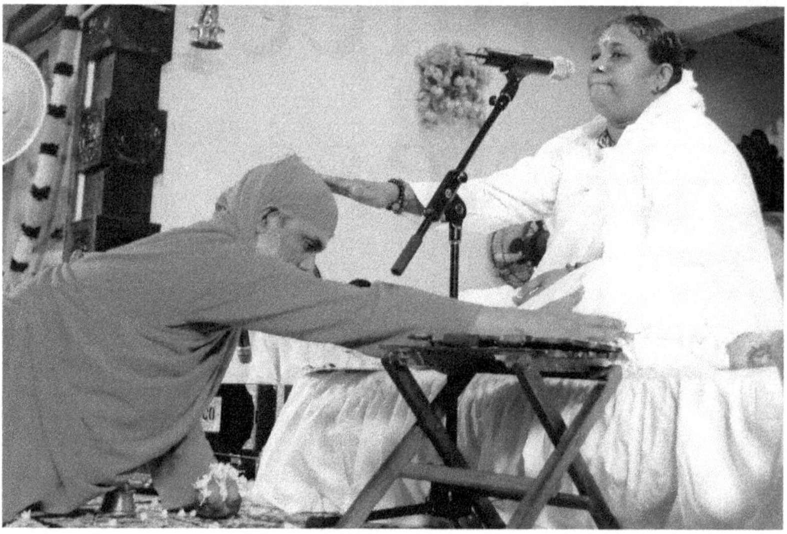

amṛtēṣvari pādam vandē

Prostrations at Amma's holy feet.

Contents

Pronunciation Guide

Vowels can be short or long:
a – as 'u' in but
ā – as 'a' in far
e – as 'a' in may
ē – as 'a' in name
i – as 'i' in pin
ī – as 'ee' in meet
o – as in oh
ō – as 'o' in mole
u – as 'u' in push
ū – as 'oo' in hoot
ṛ – as ri in rim
ḥ – pronounce 'aḥ' like 'aha,' 'iḥ' like 'ihi,' and 'uḥ' like 'uhu.'

Some consonants are aspirated (e.g. kh); others are not (e.g. k). The aspiration is part of the consonant. The examples given below are therefore only approximate.
k – as 'k' in 'kite'
kh – as 'ckh' in 'Eckhart'
g – as 'g' in 'give'
gh – as 'g-h' in 'dig-hard'
ṅ – as 'ng' in 'sing'

c – as 'c' in 'cello'
ch – as 'ch-h' in 'staunch-heart'
j – as 'j' in 'joy'
jh – as 'dgeh' in 'hedgehog'
ñ – as 'ny' in 'canyon'

The letters d, t, n with dots under them are pronounced with the tip of the tongue against the roof of the mouth, the others with the tip against the teeth.

ṭ – as 't' in 'tub'
ṭh – as 'th' in 'lighthouse'
ḍ – as 'd' in 'dove'
ḍh – as 'dh' in 'red-hot'
ṇ – as 'n' in 'naught'
p – as 'p' in 'pine'
ph – as 'ph' in 'up-hill'
b – as 'b' in 'bird'
bh – as 'bh' in 'rub-hard'
m – as 'm' in 'mother'
y – as 'y' in 'yes'
r – as 'r' in Italian 'Roma' (rolled)
ḷ – as 'l' in 'like'
v – as w in 'when'
ṣ – as 'sh' in 'shine'
ś – as 's' in German 'sprechen'
s – as 's' in 'sun'
h – as 'h' in 'hot'

With double consonants the initial sound only is pronounced twice:

cc – as 'tc' in 'hot chip'

jj – as 'dj' in 'red jet'

The 'ऽ' sign has been used when the vowel 'a' has been elided. For example, the word '*śivōऽham*' is a compound of '*śivaḥ*' and 'aham.' When these words are conjoined, the initial vowel in 'aham' is elided, and the elision is indicated by the 'ऽ' sign.

Preface

Amṛta Cintanam

Unusually heavy rains preceded Amma's arrival in Bangalore for the annual Brahmasthānam Temple[1] Festival in March 2013. The showers were a blessing, cooling the air and making the weather pleasant. Dust stopped drifting. The mud settled well on the ground. The trees that had been coated by layers of brown dust became clean and green again.

That was the year I started the '*Amṛta Cintanam*' weekly newsletter. '*Amṛta Cintanam*' loosely translates as 'Immortal Thoughts.' The newsletter was envisaged as a reflection on Amma's teachings. Initially, it was intended primarily for Amma's young children and their parents. Certain incidents had made me realize that both Indian youth and their parents lacked a firm foundation in the ancient Indian culture or scriptures. So, I researched books, including preliminary texts on Vēdānta, and books on the history of ancient India and her present social, cultural and spiritual condition. I wrote articles, edited them and emailed an article every Saturday night so that Amma's devotees could read them on Sundays. In preparing each article, I realized that the articles were relevant not only to Indians or to youth

---

1 Literally, 'place of Brahman (the Supreme Reality),' the name of the temples Amma has consecrated in various parts of India and in Mauritius. The temple shrine features a unique four-faced idol that symbolizes the unity behind the diversity of divine forms.

but to a much wider audience. Amma's teachings are universal, and therefore, their appeal is also universal. They are like leaves on the evergreen tree of spirituality.

Then the most unpleasant thing happened: a conspiracy to defame Amma and Her *āśram* (monastery) was hatched. Shortly after the conspiracy became public, Amma said during a talk in Pālakkāṭ, Kēraḷa, "Children, Amma eats only once a day!" For Her children, this humble disclosure was painful to hear. Those of us who have lived close to Amma for years know how utterly simple and self-sacrificing She is; Her abstemious eating habits epitomize Her austere life.

At first, I felt that there was nothing much I could do to help clear the air. I sought consolation in Amma's words. For me, as for Her children all over the world, Her teachings are a balm and a beacon of spiritual light, powerfully leading one ever closer to the Truth. By Amma's inspiration, I felt that I should continue writing the weekly Amṛta Cintanam articles. In my own small way, I wanted to spread the light of Amma's teachings to more and more people.

The best comes out when it emerges from the depth of one's heart. Those who have composed bhajans for Amma have this experience—that we produce the best when our minds are free from all other distractions, when our hearts are full of Amma. Then She writes, composes and sings through us!

A few years have passed since I first started writing the articles. When I look back at what I have written, I cannot help but feel amazed. I consider myself an ordinary person. How could someone like me have penned these elevating thoughts?

Suddenly, I realized with a thrill that the place where I sit to write the articles—my room on the first floor of the Bangalore āśram—is the very place Amma sat for more than two hours while recording new bhajans in 2013. And the desk on which I wrote all the Amṛta Cintanam articles was the very desk that had been kept in front of Amma, on which Her bhajan books and song sheets were placed while Her singing was being recorded. Surely, it was Her subtle touch that roused the flow of reflections on Her teachings.

By Her grace, *Amṛta-kṛpa*, this cascade of reflections has been rich and rewarding. With utmost humility, I would like to share with readers these musings, which include articles previously published in *Matruvani.*

THE SPIRITUAL MASTER

Five Gurus

It is impossible to depict fully a divine personality like Amma. Suppose I take you to the seashore and say, "This is the Indian Ocean." What I would have shown you, and what you would have seen, would have been only a tiny part of the vast ocean. To get a broader view, one must fly high into the sky in an aircraft and look at the ocean from there. Even then, one would only see the ocean's surface, not its depths. Similarly, to get a glimpse of the infinite nature of a Satguru[2] like Amma, we must go beyond the mind and its limited understanding.

Just as our view of the ocean is a limited one, our understanding of Amma is also partial. Some know Amma only as a good bhajan singer. Like those who go to the beach just to enjoy the sea breeze, these devotees listen to Amma's bhajans and leave, feeling elevated and blissful.

Others go to the beach to swim and enjoy themselves in the water. Likewise, some approach Amma for solutions to their worldly problems, and then return fulfilled.

Yet others go to the ocean to fish. Such people may be compared to devotees who come to Amma in the hope of acquiring *siddhis* (occult powers) or miraculous experiences.

Only a few dive deep to the ocean bed in search of precious gems. Rare, too, is the devotee who asks Amma for God-realization.

---

2 Literally, 'true master;' one who, while still experiencing the bliss of the Self, chooses to come down to the level of ordinary people in order to help them grow spiritually.

She is capable of elevating us from our limited body-mind consciousness to universal consciousness. During this elevation, She assumes different roles, each of which will help us progress along the spiritual path to our ultimate destination, God-realization. These roles, described in the *Guru Gītā*, are as follows:

1. *Sūcaka Guru*—one who gives or teaches us the A - Z of worldly knowledge.

Even though Amma does not have even a high-school certificate, She is a storehouse of knowledge. Many years ago, a doctor from North Kēraḷa visited Amṛtapuri. Just before his turn for darśan came, one of the *sanyāsīs* (monks) told him that Amma had been complaining about a severe headache half an hour before. The doctor, an allopath, also had a fair knowledge of acupressure, the science of healing by activating pressure points on the palms and feet. When he reached Amma, he prostrated before Her, and started pressing certain points on Her feet. Amma smiled and told him that he was pressing the wrong points! She then indicated a few other points. The doctor was confused but obeyed Amma meekly. When he returned home and consulted his book, he found, much to his astonishment, that he had been wrong and Amma, right!

2. *Vācaka Guru*—one who teaches us what our different duties are.

A few months after I joined the āśram, the brahmacārīs[3] and some devotees were working on the construction of the main āśram building. At 10 a.m., Amma came down from Her room for darśan. All of us ran to Her, but She sternly ordered the brahmacārīs to return to work. She then invited the devotees who had been helping us, into the darśan hut. Feeling sad, we went back to the construction work.

That night, after supper, Amma called all of us. In a voice full of affection, She said, "Children, Amma knows you felt sad when She asked you to return to work. Remember, Amma is not just this body. You must look upon the entire āśram as Amma's body, be attached to it and serve it."

Hearing this, a doubt entered my mind. I had studied Vēdānta[4] from an āśram in Mumbai. I thought, "Serving the āśram is well and good, but isn't any attachment a bondage? Did I leave hearth and home only to get attached to another?" With this disturbing thought in mind, I went to sleep.

The next morning, during meditation, I was still feeling agitated by that thought. After some time, Amma entered the meditation hall, sat down and guided us in our meditation. After meditation, Amma reiterated the advice She had given us the night before. She then gazed at me steadily for a few seconds and said, "Attachment to the Guru and the Guru's āśram is *not*

3 A brahmacārī is a celibate male disciple who practices spiritual disciplines under a Guru's guidance. (Brahmacāriṇi is the female equivalent.)

4 'The end of the Vēdas.' It refers to the Upaniṣads, which deal with the subject of Brahman, the Supreme Truth, and the path to realize that Truth.

bondage! We use one thorn to remove another. Attachment to the Guru removes every other attachment and takes you to Liberation. The Guru represents the whole universe. Serving the Guru is equal to serving the whole universe, just as by serving the Prime Minister, one is indirectly serving the whole country."

3. *Bōdhaka Guru*—one who initiates the disciple into a *mantra.*

The mantra that the Guru gives purifies one's inner being and brings out one's latent talents.

During my school and college days, I used to win prizes in singing competitions. I would also attend concerts of popular movie singers. Sitting among the audience, I would pray, "O Dēvī, bless me so that I can also become a movie singer one day and be able to sing on stage."

After joining Amma's āśram, receiving a mantra from Her and chanting it devoutly and regularly, I started composing bhajans—writing, scoring and singing them. I myself was surprised! I have not learnt music at all. In Chennai, when my family's neighbor, a *Carṇātic*[5] musician, heard my bhajans, he was impressed and asked my family members where I had learnt music. When they told him I had not learnt music at all, he was surprised. He asked, "Then how can he compose tunes like this?" They replied that it was by Amma's grace alone.

Most of the senior swāmis, brahmacārīs and brahmacāriṇīs who compose bhajans have not learned music but they are able to compose by divine grace.

5 Pertaining to the classical music of South India.

Now, during the annual Brahmasthānam temple festival in Chennai, movie singers come to sing for Amma. And when we sing, they listen to us!

I once had an opportunity to sing a bhajan before a famous Indian singer. He asked me who taught me music. I told him that it was Amma, none else. He was amazed, to say the least!

4. *Vihita Guru*—one who gradually makes the disciple understand the impermanence of worldly objects.

An elderly devotee recently told me, "Amma solved a serious problem I had. I used to feel ashamed that even at the age of 62, I was attracted to other women despite having a wonderful and virtuous wife. After my wife and I went for darśan together, I am now able to look upon even my wife as my sister!" A kind word, loving touch or even a look from Amma is enough to purify us and turn us towards God, the only permanent object.

5. *Tāraka Guru*—one who helps the disciple realize that every being is essentially divine, just as the waves and ocean are, in essence, the same.

Through their discourses, many *ācāryas* (religious teachers) strive sincerely to make us understand the Vēdic mantra "*tat tvam asi*" ("You are That (Supreme Being)"). Amma demonstrates by Her life that "You are divine by nature."

Those who have seen Amma's Dēvī Bhāva darśan can understand this easily. Before Dēvī Bhāva begins, She sings bhajans with a lot of devotion, like a helpless human being: "*Etrayō nāḷāyi kātirikkunnu jñān, vyarthāmāyīḍumō jīvitam iśvara…*" ("How long have I been waiting for You, O Lord. Will my life become purposeless…"). After that, She wears Dēvī's sari, crown and ornaments. Her mood changes completely. She manifests Her divinity and is no longer a helpless individual but the powerful Goddess Herself. Thus, through Her actions, She teaches us that it is possible for every human being to manifest the divine nature lying dormant within us.

While Amma manifests both the 'ordinary' and the 'divine,' Her every action demonstrates that She sees everthing as divine. One simply has to watch Her give darśan—receiving all equally and loving each one wholly. Further, when She arrives on stage She bows down to everyone, and says as much: "I bow down to all, who are the embodiments of love and the supreme self." She even prostrates to the *pīṭham* (seat), before sitting on it.

Atom Jñāna versus Ātma Jñāna[6]

A bright young Brāhmin boy was studying in a *Gurukula.*[7] He was his teacher's favorite student, being the first and best in everything. This made the other brahmacārīs of the Gurukula jealous. They tarnished his good name by alleging that he was having an illicit relationship with the teacher's wife. When the teacher heard this, he expelled the brahmacārī from the Gurukula. The brahmacārī returned home, crushed by this unexpected turn of events. When his father learned that he had incurred his Guru's wrath, he asked his son to leave home. Later, when the villagers came to know about the incident, they also spurned him. Thus, disowned by his Guru, parents and his community, he walked sadly into a forest.

Gradually, his sadness turned into intense hatred against all those who had treated him unfairly. He became vindictive. "I will punish the wrongdoers by destroying them!" Thus, the young, brilliant and kind-hearted brahmacārī became Angulimālā,[8] a cruel and powerful dacoit.

Angulimālā's teacher was a Śīkṣa Guru, who had only book knowledge but not the capacity to see Angulimālā's innocence. But when Angulimālā met the Buddha, he was transformed

---

6 Jñana = Knowledge

7 Literally, the clan (kula) of the preceptor (Guru); traditional school where students would stay with the Guru for the entire duration of their scriptural studies.

8 The name derived from the garland he wore; it was strung with the fingers (anguli) of the victims he robbed.

into a wholly new person. At a glance, Śrī Buddha understood everything about Angulimālā, and by His powerful, penetrating and compassionate gaze, He transformed Angulimālā into a serene monk, Ahimsaka.

Amma is such a Guru, just like the Buddha and Sage Vasiṣṭha. The latter was both a Śīkṣa and Dīkṣa Guru. He was not only a vast ocean of learning but also an *ātma jñānī*, a knower of the Self, who was also capable of enlightening His disciples. Amma, too, has helped us realize Her all-knowing nature on many occasions. For example, scientists and ministers meeting Amma are invariably amazed at Her expert knowledge and spiritual wisdom.

In the world, we usually measure the superiority or greatness of a person by what he or she possesses. Those who have more are considered superior to those who have less! This is like considering a person with a pair of golden crutches and gold-rimmed spectacles superior to a person who does not have them! We forget that the latter has a healthier pair of legs and eyes!

The world accepts me for what I *have*; Amma accepts me for what *I am*. The world accepts one who has plenty of money, power, position, name and fame. Amma accepts one, beholding the divinity within that person. For this reason, Amma accepts everyone because She sees divinity in every being. She knows that the body and mind are only costumes. The Guru is the only person to whom we can reveal our innermost secrets and feel assured that She will accept us even if we are the worst sinners, because She sees the divinity latent in us. She also has the power to wash away our impurities.

When gold appears in a particular form, we call it a necklace; when it appears in other forms, we call it variously a bangle, ear-ring or nose ring. There is no such 'thing' as necklace, bangle or ear-ring. All three are essentially different forms of gold. So, too, all the countless forms in this universe are only different manifestations of that Supreme Being. That eternal changeless principle is called *sat*, and the Divine Power who takes us from the *asat* (changing forms) to the changeless sat is called the Sat-guru. Amma is a Satguru.

Physics and chemistry have analyzed matter to the energy level. When scientists say that the entire universe is nothing but energy that can neither be created nor destroyed, we believe them immediately. But when the Vēdas say that the entire universe is Parāśaktī, the Almighty Power that pervades the universe, we think it is unscientific.

A 10-year-old boy heard his father, a chemistry professor, teach his students, "Every object in the universe is constituted of only atoms and energy." Once, when a wooden chair in the house broke, the father was not very upset, but when his ring was misplaced, he became visibly upset. The son innocently asked him, "Dad, when the wooden chair broke, you were not upset, but when you lost a small ring, you became agitated. Didn't you say that everything in this world is made up only of atoms and energy?"

"Shut up, you little rascal!" the father retorted. His knowledge of chemistry did not come to his rescue in day-to-day life. Real knowledge is not just information but that which brings about a personal transformation.

Consider the advantage of *ātma jñāna*—knowledge of the Self. During the early days of the āśram, Br. Rāmakṛṣṇa (now Swāmi Rāmakṛṣṇānanda) used to visit the āśram frequently. He was then working as a bank officer. One evening, when he was sitting with Amma, a middle-aged woman came to Amma and told Her, "Amma, my daughter's marriage is fast approaching. But I don't have any money."

Amma immediately got up, went inside Her house, brought a gold necklace, gave it to the devotee, and said "You can sell this necklace and use the money for the marriage!"

As the woman was walking away happily, Br. Rāmakṛṣṇa told Amma, "Amma, that's an expensive necklace. People offer this type of necklace as collateral for borrowing money!"

Immediately, Amma loudly called out to the woman. Br. Rāmakṛṣṇa thought Amma was going to take the necklace back, but to his surprise, Amma said, "Daughter, this son says that the necklace is expensive. So make sure you get a good price for it!"

Such is the benefit that ātma jñāna offers. It makes us detached from everything. Only a Satguru like Amma can bestow this knowledge on us, and thus make us truly free.

Blessed Ones

There are two types of unlucky people in this world:

1. those who have not met and been blessed by the divine power of a *mahātmā* (spiritually enlightened being). I was one such person before coming to Amma. I had read the life of Avatārs (divine incarnations) like Śrī Rāma and Śrī Kṛṣṇa, and of mahātmās like the Buddha, who transformed Angulimālā, and Upagupta, who liberated Vāsavadattā, and Śrī Rāmakṛṣṇa Paramahamsa, who created a Swāmi Vivēkānanda. I used to feel bad that I had not met, lived with or been blessed by such divine souls. Then I met Amma and realized how blessed I am, like millions of others.
2. those who have come to an Avatār or spiritual master but who still seek or are satisfied with worldly achievements. Owing to ignorance, they are not whole-hearted in their spiritual quest. They do not want freedom from the bondage of *samsāra* (cycle of births and deaths), which a Guru can bestow on them. This second type is not only unlucky but foolish, too.

Years ago, Amma told us a beautiful story. A king renounced his kingdom and became a disciple of a great Guru. When the king-turned-disciple asked for a mantra, the Guru decided to test him. While the king was meditating, another āśram resident, who was sweeping the premises, deliberately dumped dust on the king, who became furious. Seeing this, the Guru said, "You are not ready to receive a mantra!" This happened many times, and the king progressively became more and more patient.

When he had learned to control his mind, the Guru initiated him into a mantra.

From this story, we can see how difficult it is to receive a mantra from a Guru. A diamond must be given only to one who knows and appreciates its value. Nevertheless, in Her boundless compassion, Amma initiates many into a sacred mantra, giving them the opportunity to realize that the mantra is nothing less than a drop of *amṛta*, the nectar of immortality.

The king in the above story was Raja Pipa. He had an intense desire to know God, but was also attached to kingdom and power. One night, shortly after he had lain down to sleep, he heard noises on the palace roof. He called out "Who's that?"

The reply came, "We are cameleers searching for our lost camels!"

When he heard this, the king became angry and shouted, "Fools! Why would you search for camels on the roof?"

The men on the roof were actually mahātmās. One of them said, "O king, who is more foolish? We, who are looking for camels on the palace roof, or you, who seek God while lying on a silk bed of roses?"

The king was stunned. He jumped out of his bed, ran to prostrate to the holy men, and quietly left the palace in search of God. He met his Guru. After arduous *sādhana* (spiritual practice), he became a mahātmā of great spiritual realization.

From the Buddha's life, we can see how mighty kings like Bimbisāra, his son Ajātaśatru, Praśnajit and others sat at the Buddha's feet and meditated in deep silence, finally attaining *nirvāṇa* or spiritual liberation. The Buddha made all of them realize the hollowness of worldly attainments and joys.

When students matriculate in Amrita University, we try to make them understand the importance of gaining spiritual knowledge along with academic knowledge. We have seen CEOs, ministers, film stars and billionaires, among others, come to Amma for peace and solace, material wealth having failed to give them real happiness. In Amma's divine presence, they discover a new peace and joy they never knew before.

The Buddha's cousin, Dēvadatta, also a monk in Buddha's *sangha* (spiritual community), took away 500 sanyāsīs and started his own āśram, out of a desire for power. Dēvadatta's new disciples, however, realized his hollowness within a short time and returned to the Buddha. The desire for power makes one blind and takes one away from the spiritual goal.

As Amma's children, we have a right to the wealth of our Divine Mother. The *Purāṇas*[9] describe how Indra and other gods performed countless good actions, as a result of which, the Divine Mother gave them high positions in this vast universe. It also describes how the Divine Mother chastened them when they became conceited. Power is corrupting and deluding.

One of the āśram bhajans begin thus:

9 Hindu folk narratives containing ethical and cosmological teachings relating to the gods, human beings and the world. The teachings revolve around five subjects: primary creation, secondary creation, genealogy, cycles of time and history. There are 18 major Purāṇas which are designated as Śaivite (centered on Lord Śiva), Vaiṣṇavite (centered on Lord Śiva) or Śakta (centered on Dēvī).

ini oru janmam ivanēkolā kṛṣṇa
mati mōha ceḷiyil kāl iḍari vīzhum

O Kṛṣṇa, do not give me another birth
lest I fall into the deep quagmire of delusion.

During the Hyderabad Brahmasthānam Temple *pratiṣṭha* (consecration ceremony), I was fortunate to be inside the temple shrine when Amma was performing the consecration ceremony. Just when the idol was lifted and being placed on the pedestal, and Amma was blessing it, I heard sacred verses being chanted from the stage:

brahmavid āpnōti param, tadēṣābhyuktā
satyam jnānamanantam brahma
yo vēda nihitam guhāyām paramē vyōman
soȝśnute sarvān kāmān saha, brahmaṇā vipaścitēti

One who realizes Brahman attains the Supreme. With reference to that very fact, it has been declared that Brahman is Existence, Intelligence, Infinitude; one who realizes Him, hidden in the cave of the heart, enjoys supreme bliss. All his desires are fulfilled. (*Taittirīya Upaniṣad*, 2.1.1.)

The real Brahma-sthānam, i.e. abode of the Supreme, is our heart. We must become *brahmasthānārthis*, desirous of attaining the abode of Brahman.

Let us remember Amma's advice, enshrined in a bhajan:

sthāna māna dhanam ellām sthiramāṇennōrtiḍallē,
nitya vastu onnēyuḷḷu, jagadambikā

Position, prestige and wealth are all impermanent; the only Reality is the Universal Mother.

Ādi Śankarācārya[10] says,

mā kuru dhana jana yauvana garvam
hāratī nimēśat kālaḥ sarvam
māyā mayamidam akhilam hitvā
brahmapadam tvam praviśā viditvā

Never take pride in wealth, friends and youth.
Time loots all these away in a moment,
Understand that all these are the play of Māyā (cosmic delusion)
And attain the state of Supreme Bliss. (*Bhaja Gōvindam*, 11)

Śankarācārya calls it '*Brahmapadam.*' Amma calls it '*Brahmasthānam.*' Whatever belongs to the Mother belongs to Her children also.

Māyā can be explained in many ways. For example, a king is a giver, and a beggar, a receiver. Everybody wants to become a king but no one wants to give. Everyone wants to get, but no one wants to become a beggar. This is Māyā or delusion. Amma

---

10 Saint who is believed to have lived between the eighth and ninth centuries CE, and who is revered as a Guru and chief proponent of the Advaita (non-dual) philosophy, which holds that the jīva (individual soul) and jagat (universe) are ultimately one with Brahman, the Supreme Reality.

and the Buddha are beyond Māyā. They do not want to become king or queen, but they want only to give.

Let us become *vidyārthis*, seeking knowledge of the Supreme, and *abhayārthis*, seeking refuge in Amma. Amma can help us attain the Brahmasthānam, our eternal Self.

All other *sthanārthis* (desirers of position) might win some position, but it will leave them sooner or later. With the brahmasthanārthi's position, there is no competition; anyone can attain it. Having attained it, it is theirs forever.

We have been blessed to enjoy the divine presence and blessings of a Satguru. Let us not jeopardize our own spiritual life by seeking position, name and fame. Let us aim for the highest: spiritual liberation. May Amma's grace lead us to that summit!

Genuine Guru

How can we know if a Guru is genuine or not?

A man at a bus stop tried to jump into a moving bus. A passenger standing on the footboard of the bus tried to pull him inside but was not strong enough. Both fell out!

Similarly, there are many 'footboard Gurus.' Those who have learned the scriptures and done a little *tapas* (austerities) try to help others, but unfortunately as time passes, they lose sight of their goal and run after name and fame, eager to increase the number of disciples and expand their āśram. Soon, they stray from the spiritual path.

One who displays siddhis need not be a Guru. The *rākṣasas* (demons) could perform great siddhis. The *Guru Gītā* says, "The genuine Guru looks upon the innumerable kinds of occult powers possessed by yōgis and *mantravādis* (magicians) as mere straw!"

There is a famous incident in Saint Jñānēśvar's life. One day, Cāngdēv, a great yōgi, came riding on a ferocious tiger to see and impress Jñānēśvar. The saint, who was sitting with his sister and brothers on a wall, deflated Cāngdēv's ego by making the wall fly in the air towards Cāngdēv.

The *Guru Gītā* says "By whose mere glance or presence one attains calmness, peace of mind and cheerfulness—such a one is a *Param* (Supreme) Guru."

Our beloved Amma is one such Guru. This is the experience of thousands of Amma's devotees who come to Her with a long list of problems. In Her divine presence, we forget everything else.

An old friend came with his wife for Amma's darśan many years ago. He was feeling sad because he had no children even after eight years of marriage. During darśan, he told Amma his problem just once. Thereafter, he became involved in āśram activities and completely forgot his sorrow. One day, Amma asked him to bring a *kadaḷipazham*, a type of plantain that is small and sweet. She blessed the plantain and asked him and his wife to eat it. Within a year, a son was born to them.

The greatest miracle a Satguru performs is transforming the life of a devotee. Amma does it every day to thousands of devotees. In Her presence, the devotee feels full and complete. The Guru is *pūrṇa*, full and complete, like the full moon, and is capable of elevating disciples and devotees to that level also.

In *Bhaja Gōvindam*, Śankarācārya wryly notes, "*Udara nimittam bahukṛta vēṣaḥ*" ("different types of guises for the sake of the stomach"). There are many who smear themselves with *vibhūti* (sacred ash) and/or *kumkum* (saffron powder), and wear different types of *mālās* (necklaces), thus giving an impression of being great Gurus.

"Appearances are deceptive" – so goes the saying. The demon Rāvaṇa looked like a venerable sage when he came in disguise to kidnap Sītā Dēvī. On the other hand, Sage Agastya, one of the greatest sages that ever lived, was a dwarf. Another great sage, Aṣṭavakra, was a cripple. Yet another, who narrated the

Mahābhārata[11] to a gathering of saints, was Śukadēv, a 16-year-old stripling.

In the mid 90s, when we went with Amma to Mathura, the birth place of Lord Kṛṣṇa, we visited the very spot where Vasudēva, Kṛṣṇa's father, had been jailed. A priest was there, holding a garland. I was standing right behind Amma. I gestured to him to garland Amma, who even lowered Her head. But he did not, presumably because Amma was dressed simply in white. When he saw me—I was in yellow robes then—he tried to garland me probably because he was taken in by the monastic garb. Such is the erroneous vision of some people.

The word '*guru*' has many meanings. One meaning is 'very heavy'—the Guru is full of peace and joy. When we look at the pictures of God-realized saints, we see that they have a majestic appearance very unlike the magisterial look of kings and queens or political leaders, who lose their air of eminence when they are no longer in power. Such power comes from outside and is therefore impermanent, whereas the source of a mahātmā's glory lies within—a power that is spiritual and permanent.

If we gaze at Amma's photos, we will see that She has an aura of peace and splendor. This has nothing to do with the many institutions She manages. When I first came to Amṛtapuri in 1985, it was a tiny āśram with no institutions. But even then, She had that unmistakeable aura of spiritual splendor. It comes from within Her.

---

11 Ancient Indian epic that Sage Vyāsa composed, depicting the war between the righteous Pāṇḍavas and the unrighteous Kauravas.

When Amma visited Kōlkaṭa, West Bengal, for the first time, some of those accompanying Her wanted to visit Dakṣinēśvar, where Mother Kāḷī (also known as Bhavatāriṇī) had danced and given darśan to Śrī Rāmakṛṣṇa Paramahamsa. One group of devotees declared that they would not go anywhere without Amma. The second group was ready to go without Amma.

I was in the second group. We went to Dakṣinēśvar. When we returned, Amma made us understand that what we did was wrong; we should not go anywhere without our Guru. We felt sad. My understanding was that it is for seekers like us to visit sacred places; Amma has no need for such pilgrimages. Secondly, I felt that Amma should never be taken to a place where people do not appreciate Her.

The first group wanted to see Dakṣinēśvar and requested Amma to go there. She agreed, and finally, we all went together to Dakṣinēśvar.

What happened there was exactly what I had feared. In North India, there are many '*Mātājis*' (Holy Mothers), and the crowd at Dakṣinēśvar considered Amma just one among them. We went to the Bhavatāriṇī Temple and stood before the Kāḷī Shrine where Śrī Rāmakṛṣṇa Paramahamsa had worshipped. The temple priest waved the āratī lamp to Kāḷī inside the temple, and then brought the āratī lamp to Amma, who received the āratī with utmost humility and reverence. Seeing this, I could not help thinking: *if only the priest could see that the very Bhavatāriṇī whom he had been worshipping for years had come before him in flesh and blood!*

The same thing happened when Amma visited Vṛndāvan[12] in 2016. On the eve of Her program, She took us to Brahma Kuṇḍ, where Lord Kṛṣṇa had given darśan to Lord Brahma, the Creator of the Universe, and where He had performed the famed *rāsa-līlā* dance[13] with His beloved *gōpīs* (milkmaids). At our host's house, we were treated to a rāsa-līlā performance by the youth of Vṛndāvan. The host then announced that those on stage were Kṛṣṇa, Rādhā and the gōpīs themselves, not just actors; that was his faith. For many of Amma's children, their conviction is that the Supreme Being who took Śrī Kṛṣṇa's form and lived in Vṛndāvan during the *Dvapara Yuga* is now with us in Amma's form.

At the end of the performance, our host invited Swāmi Amṛtaswarupānanda to perform the āratī to the dancers on the stage; he also invited two Hindi-speaking brahmacārīs. Swāmiji stood there with folded hands, as the two brahmacārīs performed the āratī. I am sure Swāmiji's mind and the minds of a few others must have gone back to the time when Amma took us to Dakṣinēśvar. Even though the hosts had dressed Amma up as Lord Kṛṣṇa, they waved the āratī lamp only to Rādhā and Kṛṣṇa on stage, not to Amma.

Lemon- and orange-flavored soft drinks might taste like fresh orange and lemon juice, but only the latter contain Vitamin C, essential for the growth of our bodies; flavored soft drinks do

---

12 Place where Lord Kṛṣṇa spent His childhood.

13 'Dance of divine love,' wherein Lord Kṛṣṇa danced with Radha and each of the other gōpīs.

not. So, too, there is an ocean of difference between Amma adorning the garb of Kṛṣṇa and others dressing up like the Lord.

A rare few intuitively recognize spiritual greatness when they see it. Many years ago, we travelled to Jamshedpur, where Amma was conducting a program in a Hanumān temple situated atop a hill. Half way up the hill is a Kāmākṣī (a form of the Divine Mother) temple. The devotees in that temple invited Amma to visit the temple on Her way down after Her program at the Hanumān temple. She agreed.

A few brahmacārīs including me went a little earlier to make arrangements for Amma's reception. It was past five p.m. when She arrived at the temple. I was standing on the right side of the priest, who was chanting the *Aṣṭōttaram* (sacred litany of 108 attributes) and offering flowers to the Goddess in the shrine. When Amma reached the shrine, the priest continued chanting, but instead of offering flowers to the idol, he started offering flowers at Amma's feet! It was a wonderful sight.

The local devotees told us later what had happened. The temple committee members had been irritated with the priest for offering flowers at 'Mātāji's' feet, and demanded an explanation from him. The pure-hearted priest told them, "I was offering flowers to the idol. But when Amma came, I saw that it was Mother Kāmākṣī Herself walking towards me! So, I offered flowers to Her, who is Parāśaktī!"

Kṛṣṇa and Amma reveal their true nature to those who have purity of mind. Even Ṛṣi Sāndīpani, who was Lord Kṛṣṇa's teacher, did not know that Kṛṣṇa was God incarnate until He went to Yama-lōka, the abode of death, and brought back to life the ṛṣi's dead son. But Ṛṣi Garga, Lord Kṛṣṇa's family preceptor, knew that Kṛṣṇa was the Supreme Being because his father, Lord Brahma, had told him so. Bhīṣma also knew because his mother, Gangā Mātā, had told him. The residents of Vraja realized that Kṛṣṇa was divine when He lifted the Gōvardhana Hill with His little finger, whereas evil-minded Kamsa and his henchmen thought that Kṛṣṇa was a mere adept at black magic, hypnotism and mesmerism!

Hanumān knew that Lord Rāma and Lord Kṛṣṇa were two forms of the Supreme Being, but he was focused on Rāma's form alone. So was Tulsīdās, who composed one extant version of the *Rāmāyaṇa.*[14] Even when he composed a *Gaṇapati Stuti* (Hymn in Praise of Lord Gaṇapati), Tulsīdās prayed for devotion to Lord Rāma:

māngat tulsīdās kar jōrē
bas hi rām sīyā mānas mōrē

O Gaṇapati, I pray to you to bless me that Lord Sītā-Rām ever dwells in my heart!

Most of Amma's devotees had previously worshipped various forms of the Divine. After meeting Amma, they have come to feel that She is the human form of the divinity that they had been worshipping all along. They now consider Amma their sole

14 A 24,000-verse epic poem on the life and times of Rāma. There are many renditions of the Rāmāyaṇa. The one composed by Tulsīdās, the Rāmcaritmanas, is very popular in many parts of India.

refuge. At the same time, we now know that forms worshipped by others are different aspects of the same divinity, and thus have no difficulty in accepting and worshipping them.

ākāśāt patitam tōyam
yathā gacchati sāgaram
sarva dēva namskāraḥ
kēśavam pratigacchati

As all raindrops falling from the sky ultimately reach the ocean, prayers offered to all gods ultimately reach the Supreme Being.

Guru Kṛpa

In 1987, while traveling with Amma to Kōzhikōḍe, Kēraḷa, we stopped in the evening to have a bath in the Bhāratapuzha, a river near the town of Shorṇūr. Amma and the brahmacāriṇis went bathing together, while the men bathed about 100 meters downriver. A poor swimmer, I accidentally slipped into a deep and swiftly flowing part of the river and was about to drown. A few brahmacārīs were standing a few feet away, but something told me that if I called out to them, they would not be able to save me. Instinctively, I cried out "Amma!" Just as I had imagined, the brahmacārīs around me thought I was joking, and nobody came to my rescue. Amma, however, understood Her son's cry of distress and called out, "Catch hold of Satyātma (my previous name)!" It was only then the brahmacārīs understood the gravity of the situation and saved me.

After I got out of the water, I remembered what an astrologer had told me years before: "Beware, young man! Your death may be caused by drowning."

The moment Amma entered the river, it became the holiest *tīrtham* (sacred waters), and upon entering the river, I was purified and saved from death.

The Guru's presence is the holiest tīrtham. Once, a group of devotees went on a pilgrimage to all the holy rivers in India. Ēknāth, the famous saint of Mahārāṣṭra, decided to teach those devotees about the powerful presence of a mahātmā. He gave them his walking stick and said, "Please dip this into the Ganges when you bathe, and then bring it back to me."

The devotees agreed, but when one of them dipped the stick into the river, it slipped from his hands and was carried away by the swift current of the river. When the devotees returned to Ēknāth's house, they sadly reported what had happened. Ēknāth smiled, got up, walked over to the dirty pond in front of his house, and retrieved from it the same stick the Ganges had washed away!

A mahātmā's divine presence is purifying. His or her divine qualities replace our age-old negative qualities. The *Skanda Purāṇa* says:

> *satya tīrtham kṣamā tīrtham tīrtham indriyanigrahaḥ*
> *sarvabhūta dayā tīrtham tīrthanām satyavāditā jñāna*
> *tīrtham tapastīrtham kathitam sapta tīrthakam.*
>
> Knowledge of the Self, patience, sense control, kindness to all beings, speaking the truth, spiritual studies, austerities—these are the seven most sacred tīrthams.

One can acquire such qualities very easily in the presence of a God-realized being like Amma. Once we come to such a Satguru, we need not even study the scriptures, provided we are able to surrender totally to Her and implicitly obey Her. Every word the Satguru utters is scripture. The Satguru teaches more by practice than by precept. We must be very conscious, alert and watchful.

The qualities of the Satguru, who is a *siddha* (one who has accomplished the goal), become the practice of the *sādhaka* (one who is trying to accomplish). Compassion is natural to Amma; for us, it is a sādhana requiring a great deal of effort. The same holds true for calmness of mind, a constant smile, etc.

Spiritual Power

The *Rāmāyaṇa* and the *Purāṇas* narrate the story of King Kauśika, who, along with his huge army, reached the forest hermitage of Sage Vasiṣṭha after a long hunt. The sage lived with the celestial cow Kāmadhēnu (also known as Surabhī) in his āśram. This cow had the magical power of creating anything in any amount. Using this power, the sage commanded Kāmadhēnu to give the king and his army a sumptuous feast. After the feast, the king greedily asked the sage for the divine cow. In response, the sage politely replied that if Gō-*mātā* (Mother Cow) was willing to leave, the king could take her. But she wanted to stay with the sage in his āśram, just as Sītā, Lord Rāma's consort, preferred to remain with Him in the forest.

Lord Rāma and His Guru, Sage Vasiṣṭha, were both formidable spiritual powers. Kāmadhēnu was an incarnation of Mahālakṣmī, the divine consort of Lord Viṣṇu, the Preserver of the Universe. Sītā's and Kāmadhēnu's allegiance to their masters indicates that prosperity truly belongs to and remains with one who is selfless and who lives only for the welfare of the world.

To return to the story, King Kauśika became furious and tried to take Kāmadhēnu forcibly. The divine cow conjured a powerful army that routed the king and his army. Humiliated, the king returned to his palace, performed severe tapas, gained knowledge of how to use divine weapons, returned to Sage Vasiṣṭha's āśram, and attacked him with these divine weapons. But Sage Vasiṣṭha's *yōga daṇḍa* (staff that yōgis use in meditation) absorbed every *astra* (weapon), including the most powerful *Brahma-astra* that the king unleashed. It was then that King Kauśika realized the great truth: *'Dhig balam kṣatriya balam, brahma tējō balam, balam'* – 'Very insignificant, inferior and limited is military power or physical power compared to divine power acquired through austerities; that power is infinite in nature.'

A truly wise person never believes in the supremacy of material power. Sītā's father Janaka was one such example. He was the best disciple of Guru Yajñavalkya. The other disciples thought the Guru favored Janaka because the latter was king. To make the disciples aware of Janaka's greatness, Yajñavalkya contrived the following incident: during the usual scriptural class, a soldier suddenly barged in and said that Mithilā, Janaka's royal city, was going up in flames. The other disciples ran out at once to salvage their personal belongings, but King Janaka remained calmly seated and requested his Guru to continue the class. When the Guru asked Janaka why he was not anxious about his burning city, Janaka serenely replied:

anantam bata mē vittam
yasya me nāsti kiñcana
mithilāyām pradīptāyām na mē
dahyati kiñcana.

Infinite indeed is my wealth
Of which nothing is mine.
If Mithilā is burnt,
Nothing that is mine is burnt. (*Mahābhārata*, *Śāntiparva*, VII.1)

He had no attachment to his vast and wealthy kingdom, which is perishable, because he had the greatest wealth within him – imperishable spiritual power. The Indian *Tantra* and Buddhists tradition contain beautiful mantras: '*Ōm maṇī padmē hum*' and '*Om vajra sattva hum.*' Both mantras indicate that in the human heart (shaped like a lotus bud) lies the *maṇī* (gem) or *vajra* (diamond, the costliest jewel in the world) – the spark of divine consciousness. We must manifest that power through spiritual practices. The diamond is known for its absolute purity; so, too, is the *Ātma* (Self) – it is absolutely pure. The diamond is the only thing that can cut glass, but nothing can cut the diamond except itself. So, too, knowledge of the Atma is the highest.

When the Buddha returned to his hometown after enlightenment, his father, King Sudhōdhana, went to see him. The king angrily shouted, "You are a disgrace to our family. Our forefathers were all kings and we know only how to give. And you, you are begging in the streets!"

The Buddha remained calm and looked steadily into his father's eyes. The king could not return the powerful and penetrating gaze. The Buddha said, "Father, you may have immeasurable wealth, but you do not have even a moment's peace. You and your ministers are ever restless and anxious about your own security! But penniless as I am, there is none in this world who feels as secure and peaceful as I do!" The king had no answer to that.

During Amma's younger days, while steeped in tapas, a young atheist came to stab Her with a knife. Amma calmly replied, "You can kill this body of mine, but you cannot touch me!" It was the attacker himself who then collapsed in pain, as if someone had stabbed him in the chest. Physical might always fails before true spiritual power.

In 2013, rowdies harassed three high-school girls, who were devotees of Amma, near Her Bangalore āśram. Amma was informed and a complaint registered with the police. I asked some older female devotees if they could learn martial arts like kung fu or karate, and then teach the younger girls self-defense techniques. Unfortunately, all of them had back pain! I was undeterred. I had learned *kaḷari payaṭṭu*, the martial arts of Kēraḷa, a long time ago, and though I was out of touch, I decided to teach the girls myself. I summoned them, their parents and the boys from the Bangalore āśram, and taught them all *Sūrya Namaskār*, the Sun Salutation series of yoga *āsanas* (postures). I reminded them that the power that really protects is the power of mantras. So, on Sundays and Thursdays, we did a lot of chanting, and on the other five days, I taught them what little self-defense techniques I knew. I believe it was good enough to benefit them in dangerous situations. Alas, the training lasted only for eight months or so; I myself had a minor slip disc and back pain after that! Perhaps, Amma preferred that Her children rely on spiritual power. After all, it was devotion and not physical prowess that had saved Sītā, Draupadī, Prahlāda and many others. When the time comes, I felt sure that Amma Herself would teach us self-defense techniques in some way. By Her grace, a woman devotee introduced us to karate instructors in Bangalore.

Amma has now given our youth Her blessings and permission to start learning self-defense techniques.

And yet, to conclude that spirituality does not give any importance to physical defense is foolish. After winning the battle of Kalinga, King Aśōka was filled with remorse when he saw hundreds of thousands of soldiers lying dead on the battlefield. He converted to Buddhism and started practicing non-violence. When he converted, the entire population in his kingdom also converted with the result that after his death, enemies conquered his kingdom.

King Aśōka's attitude had been wrong. When tyrant kings and their armies harassed peaceful Buddhist monks, Bōdhi Dharma, a master from South India, went to China and taught them kaḷari payaṭṭu, which later became kung fu, karate, etc. This fact is recorded by the Shao-Lin monastery in China. When Mughal soldiers harassed sanyāsīs in North India, Swāmi Madhusūdana Saraswatī of the Śankarācāya Order met the then Mughal emperor Akbar and asked him to intervene. Akbar said he was helpless and requested the swāmi to create a combat force. Thus arose the *Akhāḍas* or training centers, where sanyāsīs were trained in tough spiritual practices, even tougher physical combat, and the use of weapons. They came to be known as *nāga sanyāsīs*.

Years ago, during a Brahmasthānam festival in Hyderabad, after performing ārati to Amma one morning and offering flowers at Her sacred feet, I was surprised when Amma smiled mischievously at me, stretched Her hand, and put something in my two cupped hands: it was a piece of nail from one of Her thumbs! It looked like a tiny sword. Back in my room, I put it in my little kumkum box. I remembered Lord Narasimha,[15] who had torn Hiraṇyakāśipu apart with His divine nails. Hiraṇyakāśipu had obtained a boon whereby no weapon could kill him. Narasimha's nails were the answer! I also remembered how Goddess Durgā appeared before Chhatrapati Śivāji and gave him a sword, which led him to victory. Durgā also appeared before Swāmi Vidyāraṇya and blessed him, enabling him to establish the Vijayanagar Empire.

In spiritual life, a sādhak's sword is discernment, which cuts asunder all attachments. This is what the *Bhagavad Gītā* teaches, too – '*asanga śastrēṇa dṛḍhēna chitvā*' ('with the sharp ax of non-attachment') (15.3).

Years ago, after learning kaḷari payaṭṭu, I had become good in self-defense, but I still had a little fear. Chanting Amma's mantra for many years has now made me much more fearless even though I do not have much ability to defend myself physically anymore! Brahmacariṇis working in branch āśrams in locales where there is religious conflict have reported remaining fearless even when they received death threats over the telephone. Chanting Amma's mantra gives us infinite strength.

Let us develop physical, material and spiritual power, and develop the conviction that spiritual power alone saves.

---

15 Narasimha = literally, man-lion. A divine incarnation of Lord Viṣṇu who killed Hiranyakāśipu, the demon king who had been persecuting devotees of the Lord, including his own son Prahlāda.

EFFACING THE EGO

Luminous Like the Full Moon

It was nearing sunset. A sanyāsī was deeply immersed in meditation, his face serene and peaceful. He was unaware of the presence of a beautiful young dancer waiting impatiently for him to open his eyes. Her name was Vāsavadattā. Her stunning good looks captivated all the young men in the city. But she would entertain only the very rich. She was now fascinated by this young sanyāsī, Upagupta, who was from the Buddha's lineage.

After some time, the young sanyāsī opened his eyes slowly and then stood up. Vāsavadattā walked up to him and invited him to her house. He declined politely. All her efforts to persuade him to accept the invitation were in vain. The only response she got from Upagupta was, "I will come at the right time!" With these words, he smiled, turned around and walked away slowly and gracefully.

The dancer felt sad and humiliated. "What kind of a man is he!" she wondered. The other men in the city would have jumped at an invitation from her, whereas this monk didn't seem interested at all.

Years passed. Vāsavadattā fell prey to the dreaded disease, leprosy. Those who had adored and worshipped her would cover their noses and avert their gaze when she came near. The most hard-hearted among them threw her into a ditch outside the city.

As she lay there in pain and agony, racked by hunger and thirst and in a half-conscious state, she heard footsteps approaching her. When she looked up, she saw the sanyāsī who had turned down her invitation many years ago.

With tears in her eyes, she said, "O noble one! You snubbed me when I was attractive. Why have you come now?"

Upagupta sat down beside her. He poured water into her mouth and quenched her thirst. He said, "My child, now is the right time. I see the same you that I saw years ago. Decay and death is for the body only, my child! You are that eternal, blissful, ever-existent being. Death cannot touch you. Be peaceful and blissful." He then guided her deep into her Self. The pain and agony disappeared. Vāsavadattā passed away peacefully.

When I read this story many years ago, I wanted to meet a Guru of this caliber. In 1985, when I visited Amṛtapuri for the first time, I saw a divine being treating the wounds of a leper in a unique way: by licking the wounds. That great soul was a young *sanyāsinī* (ordained female monk), albeit one dressed in a spotless white sari, and the leper, a young man.

The wounds of leprosy are outside, and they can be healed relatively easily. The inner wounds that most of us suffer from—ego, pride, jealousy, anger and hatred, among others—are harder to heal. But Amma can clean all the suppurating wounds in leprous minds. When the impurities are removed, our real being will shine, like the luminous full moon.

Years ago, Amma narrated a thought provoking story. A man was standing on top of a hill, wearing only a loincloth. A few passersby, impressed by this 'renunciate,' asked him who he was. The man said, "Do you see that big building in blue and white? It is a company worth $500 million. I renounced that company. There is a five-star hotel worth even more than that. I renounced that, too. I'm the one who renounced so many million dollars!"

Amma was teaching us a subtle truth—that we may renounce everything, but it is difficult to renounce one's ego.

There was a demon named 'Madhu,' which means honey. It represents the ego, which we are very attached to and which we relish like honey. Amma has said that compared with removing the ego, removing the Himalayas would be child's play! Only the Guru can eradicate the ego. Her *dṛṣṭi* (look), *sparśa* (touch) and *vāk* (word) all have immense power, like laser beams that can cut even steel.

Saint Nanin from the Buddhist tradition has spoken about how his Guru reformed him. He and his fellow disciples were not allowed to sleep in the day. One day, Nanin went out to buy some things for the āśram, and when he returned, he was totally exhausted. He thought he would lie down for a while; his Guru had gone out. Without thinking twice, he lay down just inside in the doorway and fell asleep immediately. The Guru returned before Nanin awoke, and stepping inside, tripped over a sleeping Nanin. When Nanin opened his eyes, he saw his Guru standing over him. Before he could react, the Guru bent over and whispered, "I'm really sorry. I didn't mean to disturb you!"

This incident brought about a total change in Nanin's life. Never again did he sleep during the day. This example shows how the Guru can destroy our ego.

During a recent Indian tour, my bhajan session during Amma's darśan in Mumbai, Mahārāṣṭra, was slotted at the end. At the scheduled time, the bhajan group and I sat behind Amma on the stage. Just then, She asked the brahmacārī operating the sound system to play the new bhajans. He played one new bhajan after another. I waited and waited and waited. In such situations, one can learn and develop the virtue of surrender. We learn to put Amma before ourselves and our needs, whatever they may be. We learn to remain witnesses to situations.

Often, our strong individualities make us aggressive, and we strive to get things done our way. A few months ago, while at AIMS Hospital, I had an interesting conversation with an elderly devotee, who visits patients and counsels them. She spoke of a student who was suffering from depression and had committed suicide. She said, "Swāmiji, nowadays parents give their children whatever they want. These youngsters, accustomed to getting everything they want, become so upset when they don't, that they might even put an end to their lives!"

A Guru's grace and teachings are especially relevant in such situations. A Satguru is a master of circumstances, whereas we are victims. Lord Rāma was totally unaffected by what the world gave him or took away from him. He was equally happy whether in the forest or palace. Similarly, Amma's inner bliss remains unaffected by outer circumstance.

Coming back to the situation in Mumbai, I waited for an hour and 15 minutes as the new bhajans continued being played. Suddenly, Amma turned around and saw me. She gave me a look of concern and said, "Oh! Oh! Waiting to sing bhajans!" Gesturing with Her hands, She asked the sound system brahmacārī to stop playing the bhajans, and then motioned for me to start singing.

For a few minutes, I sat there, petrified and reflecting on Amma's actions. I knew that they could be interpreted in two ways:

1. Out of motherly compassion, She was feeling sorry for me, who had been waiting so long to sing. Amma was also showing Her humility. She has said that one should have the humility to bow down even before an ant; only then one can reach the Supreme Being.
2. Indirectly, She was teaching me to be patient and humble enough to wait indefinitely. Suppose I had to wait until the end of darśan without receiving an opportunity to sing. A true seeker would accept the situation without becoming upset. Being able to see Amma was already a big blessing; in fact, it is the greatest blessing!

We forget that Amma is *pañcavaktra*, one with five faces, and also *viśvatōmukhī*, one who is facing all directions at the same time, like a flame. She was watching me, even though Her physical face was turned away from me and the others sitting behind Her. Most of us have this delusion, that Amma looks at us only when Her face is turned towards us. Amma is watching us all the time; She knows our every thought.

The 'I' Specialist

In China and Southeast Asian countries, the Divine Mother is known as Kuan Yin, the Goddess of Compassion. In one of Her incarnations, She was born as the youngest daughter of a very cruel king in a Chinese state. In Her family, She was the only compassionate one; the rest, including Her older brothers and sisters, were cruel and jealous of Her popularity among the masses. They made many unsuccessful attempts to do away with Her. When the cruel king became afflicted with disease and insomnia as a result of his wicked actions, the cunning brothers and sisters of the princess coerced the royal physician to prescribe a radical remedy for the cure of the king: soup brewed from the eyes and hands of a virgin princess. The youngest princess was the only one available, and She readily agreed to sacrifice Her eyes and hands for the sake of Her father. The king was healed. But a great miracle also took place: She received new eyes and a thousand hands, and ascended to heaven.

The symbolic meaning of this story is that if we serve the world selflessly with our hands and heart, the whole world will come to revere us and thus become a haven for us.

The *Śiva Purāṇa* contains the story of how Dakṣa, the king of created beings, once became angry with Lord Śiva, his son-in-law. Dakṣa arranged a great sacrifice and invited all the important beings in the universe, except Lord Śiva, to it. Ashamed of Her father's conduct, Lord Śiva's divine consort Satī went to the sacrifice and gave up Her body in the sacrificial fire.

The allegorical significance of this story is that the real sacrifice is neither ghee nor other offerings but oneself. The 'I' or the ego alone is the real offering because the ego alone is our creation and keeps us away from God. When I offer myself to the world, the entire world looks after me.

Mother Herself says, "God, the merciful one, is waiting with outstretched hands to receive your ego. But if you will not give it, it will be taken, for only then will you be happy."

Amma is the divine surgeon who removes our ego through skillful surgery. Her maternal love is the anesthesia that prevents us from feeling the pain of Her surgery; otherwise, the amputation of the ego is very painful! She removes all the wrong notions about 'I' that have taken root in us, and reveals to us the real 'I,' which is pure consciousness, infinite bliss, and eternally free.

That is why we call Amma the world's number one 'I' specialist—because She removes the false 'I' and reveals the real 'I' in us. She opens the 'eye' of wisdom in us. Therefore, She is also the world's number one 'eye' specialist.

Snake Charmer

An elderly scholar was traveling to a distant place. As he was due to return only the next day, his wife gave him two packets of food—for lunch and dinner—which he put into his shoulder bag. He then set off. By noon, he reached the middle of a forest. He sat under a tree, opened his bag, took out his lunch and ate it. After lunch, he closed his bag and continued on his journey. He reached his destination much earlier than expected. After finishing his work there, he quickly started for home, hoping to reach home that night and have his dinner there.

On his way back, he met a dignified looking monk, who looked at him gravely and said, "If you return home today, your wife will die. If you don't return, you will die."

The scholar was shocked and speechless. Trusting that the monk's prophecy would not fail, he decided not to return home so as to save his wife from death. Resigned to the prospect of an impending death, the scholar walked slowly and cautiously, looking in all directions, expecting a wild animal to pounce on him at any moment.

After he had walked quite a distance, he came upon a group of monks sitting under a tree, listening to a discourse given by their leader. It was the Buddha!

The scholar joined the group and, after the discourse ended, made his way to the Buddha. After prostrating to Him, the scholar told Him about his meeting with the monk. He begged the Buddha to save him.

The Buddha smiled and said, "I am very hungry. Do you have something to eat?" In great joy, the scholar grabbed his shoulder bag with one hand. At that point, the Buddha asked him to hand over the bag. The scholar did so. The Buddha quietly opened the bag, put His hand inside, and pulled out a small but deadly snake.

In a flash, the scholar understood what had happened. When he had put his bag on the ground after opening it and taking out his lunch, the snake had crawled inside. So, he had been carrying death all along on his shoulders! If he had returned home, he would have handed the bag to his unsuspecting wife, who would have been stung to death when she put her hand into the bag to take out the dinner packet. If he had not gone home, the same fate would have befallen him! He realized how his good fortune had led him to the Buddha, and how the enlightened, all-knowing Master had saved him. Falling at the Buddha's feet, he wept in devotion and joy.

While traveling through the forest of human life, we expect danger from all directions and therefore try to be cautious and alert. But we don't realize that we are carrying the greatest danger that can take away our life or those of our loved ones: the poisonous snake of our ego. But we will be saved if we offer the shoulder bag of our mind to an enlightened Master, who knows our past, present and future.

In the Buddha's hand, the poisonous snake became harmless. Around Lord Śiva's neck, the dangerous snake is an ornament.

Lord Viṣṇu[16] rests peacefully on a huge serpent. And in Amma's presence, the most dangerous snake becomes harmless; our ego becomes silent.

Shortly after I first came to Amṛtapuri, one afternoon, a few brahmacārīs were sitting with Amma in front of the *kaḷari* (ancestral shrine). One of the brahmacārīs was reading aloud the episode from the *Bhāgavatam* where Sage Śamīka's son curses King Parīkṣit to die of snakebite. In search of water, Parīkṣit enters a hermitage where Sage Śamīka is immersed in meditation. He does not hear Parīkṣit's plea for water. The king loses his temper, picks up a dead snake lying nearby and places it around the sage's neck. When the sage's son returns home and sees the dead snake around his father's neck, he utters a curse: the person responsible would die within seven days.

Amma gave a beautiful explanation of the story. "Parīkṣit is the human being who wanders in the forest of human life, thirsting for peace and happiness. He enters Sage Śamīka's hermitage and asks for water, which represents knowledge. When the meditating sage does not respond, Parīkṣit loses his patience and puts a dead snake around the sage's neck. The dead snake is our dead ego, which we offer to our Guru." Thus, the story of King Parīkṣit is an allegory about an individual wandering in search of happiness and, reaching the Guru's abode, attaining total peace, happiness and freedom upon surrendering the ego. Amma, our Guru, smilingly takes our ego away in the same way that Vāmana took away Mahābali's.

---

16 Lord of Sustenance in the Hindu Trinity.

Vāmana, a small Brāhmin boy and incarnation of Lord Viṣṇu, approaches King Mahābali, emperor of the earth, while the king is conducting a ritual sacrifice and giving away gifts. He asks Mahābali for land that can be covered by three strides. Amused by the seemingly insignificant request, the king urges him to ask for more. Vāmana sticks to his request. He grows in size. With the first stride, he covers the earth and sky; with the second, the netherworlds; since Vāmana had no other place for his third step, Mahābali offers him his head. Vāmana places his foot on the king's head and pushes him into the netherworld. The story is about surrendering our pride and sense of doership, in short, our ego; for, in truth, nothing is ours, everything belongs to God.

An experience I had illustrates how Amma works to get rid of our ego. In 1987 or 1988, I composed *'Pāvana Gangē Tāyē,'* a bhajan on Mother Gangā, the personification of the Ganges River. I felt proud of it, as it was our āśram's first bhajan on Gangā. When I showed it to Swāmi Turīyamṛtānanda, he pointed out a few mistakes in the lyrics. Though I corrected the mistakes, inwardly I felt that he was a little jealous—this is how the ego works! Amma, the merciful Guru, removed my ego when, within a short time, Swāmi Turīyamṛtānanda wrote a much better bhajan on Gangā, *'Gangē Svargangē.'* Not only that, that bhajan, when scored and sung by Swāmi Amṛtaswarupānanda, outclassed the bhajan I had written!

When the Best is the Worst

It is customary for Hindu devotees to offer coconuts in temples as a form of propitiating God. They might ask, "How many coconuts should I offer?"

Amma answers, *"Tēngayallā, makkaḷē, tēngal āṇu iśvaranu vēnḍatu!"* – "Children, what God wants are not *tēngas* (coconuts) but *tēngal* (yearning)." God is pleased when we have devotion and intense desire for God's vision.

The best we can offer God is our worst. A story Amma narrates illustrates this point.

There were three brothers. The first two were well-educated and well-employed, but the youngest was spoilt. He was indifferent to his studies, a drunkard and chain smoker, and he kept bad company. Their mother's 60th birthday was approaching. The older brothers returned from Dubai, bearing rich gifts. For the first time, the youngest son felt sad and guilty because he had nothing to offer his mother. On her birthday, the older brothers presented their mother with expensive gifts. The mother, though pleased with these gifts, also felt sad for her pet son, the youngest. He came forward, knelt before his mother, placed a packet of cigarettes and a bottle of liquor in front of her, and said, "Mother, I promise that I will never again smoke or drink. This is my birthday gift to you!"

When she heard this, the mother shed tears of joy. The older brothers, who were until then reluctant to help their younger brother find a job because of his irresponsible ways, soon found him a job.

Hearing that God wants our yearning and not coconuts, the miserly may heave a sigh of relief, thinking that they need not spend money any more for God or charity. Actually, we can offer God both tēnga and tēngal—that is ideal.

Moreover, offering the coconut is symbolic. The outer shell of the coconut represents the body, the inner flesh represents the mind, and the water, the ego or *jīva*. Doing *abhiṣēkam* (ceremonial bathing) of the temple idol with coconut water symbolizes the jīva becoming one with the Lord, the *Paramātma* (Supreme Self). Also, just as the coconut conceals the unmanifest tree, the Lord is present in each one of us in unmanifest form:

> *parēṇa nākam nihitam guhāyām…*
>
> Higher than heaven, seated in the cave of the heart. (*Kaivalyōpaniṣad*, 1.1.3)

Mahātmās like Amma help us discover the divine within.

Of course, the best we can offer Amma need not always be the worst. "I will chant the *Sahasranāma* (sacred litany of thousand names) ___ many times as an offering to Amma; I will chant my mantra ___ many times as an offering to Amma." Making such resolutions and following up on them is another ideal offering. Where there is tēngal, Amma will definitely accept the tēnga or any other offering. Anything offered with devotion becomes a sacred offering. Any action performed with remembrance of God is prayer or worship.

Actually, Amma is already *pūrṇa* (complete). What can we possibly offer Her? The other question is, what do we really have that we can offer? Dēvakī, Kṛṣṇa's mother, once asked the Lord why He created sorrow. Kṛṣṇa replied, "Mother, if you ask me why I created human beings, animals, birds, plants and trees, I can tell you. If you ask me why I created the countless planets, stars and galaxies, I can tell you. But if you ask me why I created sorrow, I cannot tell you because sorrow is not my creation. It is one's own creation." It is the ego that creates sorrow. So, the only thing we can call our own is our ego. It is this alone that can we offer Amma.

The Crow Guru

During a recent Indian tour, Amma asked, "When did the crow become a Guru for Garuḍa, the eagle?"

The dialogue between Garuḍa, the vehicle of Lord Viṣṇu, and a saint in the form of a crow ('Kāka Bhuśuṇḍi') appears in the Uttara Khaṇḍa of the *Rāmcaritmanas*. Garuḍa had become very proud of his strength. He thought, "Lord Viṣṇu upholds all of creation, and I am the one who carries Lord Viṣṇu Himself." When one becomes egoistic, one's mind and vision become clouded.

During the war between Rāma's army and that of Rāvaṇa, Indrajit sent the powerful *nāgastra* (missile of snakes), which bound both Rāma and Lakṣmaṇa, and made them unconscious. Indra and the other gods requested Garuḍa to neutralize the effect of the nāgastra. Within no time at all, Garuḍa released both of them from the nāgastra. But a doubt arose in his mind. Seeing Lord Rāma lying helpless on the ground, he wondered how He could possibly be an incarnation of Lord Viṣṇu. This confusion was caused by delusion arising from pride.

Garuḍa flew to Lord Śiva and requested Him to remove his doubt. The Lord understood at once the cause of Garuḍa's delusion. He told Garuḍa, "I'm busy now. Go to Kāka Bhuśuṇḍi, who can help to remove your doubt."

Garuḍa flew to Kāka Bhuśuṇḍi, a great sage and devotee of Lord Rāma who had the form of a crow. By then, Garuḍa had realized his mistake. Though he was king of the birds, he humbly sat down before the crow to learn about Śrī Rāma's real nature. The crow is considered inferior among birds; in fact, it is called the 'scavenger bird.'

Kāka Bhuśuṇḍi then narrated his experience. He said that he also used to wonder who Śrī Rāma really was. With this doubt in mind, he had flown to the palace of Daśaratha, Rāma's father, when Rāma was only a year old. There, he had snatched away the slice of bread that infant Rāma was eating. With the bread in his beak, Kāka Bhuśuṇḍi perched on the branch of a tree, but was surprised to see baby Rāma standing beside him, stretching out his cute hands and crying for the piece of bread. Kāka Bhuśuṇḍi then flew from the earth (*bhuh*) to the higher worlds—*bhuvaḥ* (world of ancestors) and *suvaḥ* (world of the gods). To his astonishment, baby Rāma continued following him, crying and asking him for the piece of bread. Kāka Bhuśuṇḍi flew to even higher realms: *mahar lōka, janaḥ lōka, tapaḥ lōka* and, finally, *satya lōka*, the highest world and abode of Lord Brahma, the Creator of the Universe. But baby Rāma followed him even there, crying for His piece of bread! Kāka Bhuśuṇḍi realized that Śrī Rāma was none other than Lord Viṣṇu Himself, who pervades the universe, and prayed to Him to reveal His Divine form. Compassionate Rāma did so and blessed Kāka Bhuśuṇḍi.

Humbled, Garuḍa thanked Kāka Bhuśuṇḍi, and together they sang praises of Śrī Rāma. Thus filling their hearts with joy and peace, Garuḍa flew back to Vaikuṇṭha, the abode of Lord Viṣṇu.

Many years ago, we watched this televised episode of the *Rāmcaritmanas* with Amma.

On another occasion, Lord Viṣṇu sent Garuḍa to Kishkindha to fetch Hanumān, foremost devotee of Lord Rāma. Garuḍa flew there at once. When he approached Hanumān and informed him about Lord Viṣṇu's request, Hanumān denied having any knowledge of Lord Viṣṇu. As far as Hanumān was concerned, Lord Rāma was his sole refuge. When Garuḍa threatened to carry him away by force, Hanumān challenged him to go ahead. Garuḍa tried with all his might but was unable to lift Hanumān even an inch. Hanumān then coiled his tail around Garuḍa and hurled him miles away. Garuḍa returned to Lord Viṣṇu, his ego bruised but wiser. If Garuḍa, the Lord's chosen vehicle, can fall prey to egoistic feelings, it goes without saying that lesser mortals like us can, too.

Humble Leadership

The Hindu epics contain many stories of great kings who were loved and admired by their subjects because of their nobility and compassion towards them. According to the scriptures,

rājānam rāṣtrajam pāpam
rājapāpam purohitam
bhartāram strīkṛtam pāpam
śiṣyapāpam gurum vrajēt

The king is responsible for his subjects' mistakes,
the Guru for those committed by the king,
the husband for the wife,
and the Guru for the disciple.

This means that the king, Guru and husband should first practice righteousness themselves. Only then can they make their subjects, disciples and wife respectively adhere to the path of righteousness.

Among the different duties performed by human beings, those performed by the king or leader are the most difficult. To be in a high position, controlling everyone, *and* remain humble and selfless is extremely difficult for ordinary people. A Satguru's guidance is vital in this regard.

The story of King Nahuṣa in the *Mahābhārata* illustrates how even the noblest of men, when elevated to high positions, can fall as a result of the power of Māyā. The king was the most virtuous and humble ruler on earth during his time. Because of this, he was invited to rule *Dēvalōka* (world of the gods) when Indra, the presiding king, was banished as a result of a curse he incurred for bad actions.

At first, King Nahuṣa ruled Dēvalōka with humility and righteousness, but as time passed, his ego got the better of him. He wanted Indra's chaste wife for himself. When he proposed to her, she was in a dilemma. She sought the advice of the heavenly Guru, Bṛhaspati, who advised her to request Nahuṣa to come to her palace in a palanquin carried by the illustrious Seven Ṛṣis.[17] Blinded by lust, Nahuṣa ordered the Ṛṣis to carry him, and they obliged. One of the sages, Agastya, being short, could not keep pace with the other six ṛṣis, who were taller. As a result, the palanquin kept wobbling. Irritated, Nahuṣa kicked Sage Agastya and shouted "*Sarpa! Sarpa!*" ("Faster! Faster!") Sage Agastya lost his patience and cursed Nahuṣa with the words "*Sarpō bhava!*" ("May you become a snake!") (The word 'sarpa' has both meanings.) Nahuṣa fell headlong from heaven to the earth, and had to remain in a forest for a long time until the Pāṇḍavas helped him to gain liberation.

Some time ago, I read a magazine article about political leaders seeking the guidance of spiritual leaders. This is highly desirable, because only spiritual leaders like Amma can inspire political leaders to lead a life of selfless service. There is a beautiful verse composed by Adi Śankarācārya. One of the lines reads, "*Nṛpālimauli-vrajaratnakānti-saridvirājad-jhaṣakanyakābhyām.*" It describes the feet of the Satguru walking in between two rows

17 The seven most exalted sages.

of kings. The gems of the crowns of the kings prostrating to the Guru create a luminous stream in which the Guru's feet move like two fishes swimming in a river of light.

Although Amma heads many institutions, She is the very personification of selflessness, justice, humility and simplicity. Another exemplar of humility was Abraham Lincoln. Once, he transferred an army battalion from one strategic point to another. This would prove to be a grave mistake. The experienced War Secretary, Stanton, a straightforward man, remarked, "Lincoln is a fool. This is fatal mistake."

Those who were jealous of Stanton took this opportunity to create problems for him. They informed Lincoln of what Stanton had said. Lincoln was silent for some time and then asked with all seriousness, "Did Stanton call me a fool?" When the others nodded their heads, Lincoln calmly replied, "Then I certainly must be one!"

It must be noted that spiritual leaders like Amma never give their blessings in the form of lordship, power and victory to those who do not deserve them. Queen Gāndhārī, mother of the Kauravas, had acquired tremendous powers because of her chastity and purity. When Duryōdhana, the eldest of the Kauravas, came to her for blessings, she blessed him, saying, "*Yaśasvī bhava*" ("May you become famous"). Duryōdhana requested her to bless him with victory, but Gāndhārī flatly refused, saying that she could not bless him with something he does not deserve, for he was utterly selfish and unjust.

The Divine Swan

A saint was sitting outside his humble dwelling, looking towards the sky. A storm was fast approaching. A flock of birds perched on a tree was chirping excitedly. The saint opened wide the door of his barn, so that the birds could enter and take refuge in that safe sanctuary. Unfortunately, the birds either did not notice or failed to understand his gesture. With his divine powers, the saint took the form of a bird, flew towards the group of birds, mingled with them and led the flock into the barn, thus saving them from the fury of the storm.

This is what the Supreme Being does, through the form of an Avatār or Incarnation. Knowing that earthly beings are caught in the cyclone of birth, sorrow and death, He comes into their midst, often in the form of a human being, makes them see and understand the need for the 'safe barn' of His heavenly abode, and leads them there.

Among the many Avatārs of Viṣṇu, Rāma and Kṛṣṇa are the most popular because they came as human beings, behaved like human beings undergoing the joys and sorrows of worldly existence, and taught humans the invaluable lesson of detachment born of true knowledge and wisdom—in other words, how to be free *in* action, not *from* action.

We compare Rāma and Kṛṣṇa with lotuses for two reasons. Firstly, they are attractive. Secondly, they remain unaffected by the worldliness around them, like the lotuses that emerge from but remain unsullied by dirty waters.

Isn't this the lesson that not only Avatārs but every God-realized soul teaches us? Isn't it the lesson that Amma, the *Premavatār* (Incarnation of Love), is also teaching us? In his *Rāmcaritmanas*, Tulsīdās says, "God has created this universe consisting of animate and inanimate beings as a mixture of both good and evil. The swans in the form of saints know how to separate the milk of goodness from the water of evil, choosing the permanent and sentient, and rejecting the impermanent and inert."

A disciple once asked his Guru to bless him with *siddhis* (miraculous powers) like walking on water, remaining under water for a long time, and flying. The Guru laughed at the disciple and told him that fish and birds could perform these 'feats.' "The greatest siddhi," the Guru told his disciple, "is remaining in the midst of worldliness and not being affected by it." Isn't Amma, the *Jñanavatār* (Incarnation of Wisdom), in fact, demonstrating this siddhi? She is teaching us that true freedom born of wisdom isn't running away from the problems and challenges of life, but facing them and accepting victory or defeat with equanimity.

I remember a story. The Guru was sitting outside his hut looking towards the āśram's main gate. One of his disciples, a very learned and austere seeker, was pushing someone out of the āśram; it was a man who was in the habit of drinking heavily.

When the disciple returned, the Guru asked him why he had pushed the man out. The disciple replied, "Guruji, he was stinking! I think he is slightly drunk. We should not allow drunkards to enter our āśram."

"Oh, I see," the Guru replied. "But there is a stench here that's even more nauseating than the smell of liquor from that man!"

The astonished disciple asked, "What's that, Guruji?"

The Guru replied, "Your ego! It stinks more than the liquor consumed by that man. That man, having realized his weakness, was coming here for consolation and to reform himself. But you consider him impure and think of yourself as pure. If you think you are superior to others because of your learning and austerity, you have wasted your time in the āśram."

In the *Śiva Purāṇa*, Lord Śiva tells his consort Pārvatī, "There are different types of egos: the ego that comes from physical strength, from political power, from wealth and so on. But the most powerful ego, the one that is the most difficult to destroy, is the ego that comes from learning and austerity. People with such egos think, 'I know so much,' or 'I have done so much tapas.'"

Only the Guru can create situations that make us aware of our ego. It is only in the presence of a Guru, the enlightened master, that we can acquire learning, perform tapas and render service, and gain the results of all three: purity of mind and humility.

Devotion to our Guru and an awareness of the ultimate goal of human life motivate us to surrender our ego to the Guru. When our ego disappears, we become lightweight and can ascend with Her to Her heavenly abode.

Precious Circles

God incarnates on earth and lives among us like ordinary human beings. His presence is extraordinarily blissful. A few lines from the bhajan '*Kṛṣṇam Kalaya Sakhi Sundaram*' come to mind:

anganām anganām, antarē mādhavō,
mādhavam mādhavam, cāntarēṇāngaṇā

What is being described is the *rāsa līlā*, the mystic dance of Lord Kṛṣṇa and the gōpīs of Vṛndāvan. Each gōpī was dancing with a Kṛṣṇa, who had assumed as many forms as there were gōpīs. We might think, "How blessed the gōpīs were!" We are just as blessed because we have Amma with us, and She makes us all dance during festive occasions like *Ōṇam* and *Kṛṣṇa Jayantī*. That single enchanting form is enough to make us all dance in divine ecstasy.

My mind goes back to 1986, the year I joined the āśram. Imagine a lake in which a big, white lotus in full bloom is ringed by a few other white lotuses. That was how it was: Amma, in Her spotless white sari, surrounded by Her children in white—a small, divine circle. A deep and blissful silence permeated the scene. The only sounds were those of the wind and waves. I had thought then, "People talk of vicious circles; they have not seen precious circles, and here is one!" At its center was Sudhāmaṇī,[18] the gem (*maṇi*) of divine nectar (*sudhā*).

18 The name Amma's parents gave Her.

There have been other precious circles—the gōpīs around Śrī Kṛṣṇa, and the *vānaras* (monkeys) around Śrī Rāma. The *Guru Gītā* speaks of another precious circle: that of Lord Śiva, Pārvatī and their sons, Gaṇēśa and Muruga. This divine family resides on the beautiful peaks of Kailāś in the Himalayas. There, the cobra around Śiva's neck and the mouse, Lord Gaṇēśa's *vāhana* (vehicle), live in peace. The cobra has no fear of the peacock, Muruga's vāhana. Nandi, the bull, who is Śiva's vāhana, is not scared of Durgā's vāhana, the lion. It is a divine circle, a precious circle.

When Rāvaṇa, a devotee of Śiva, visited Kailāś, he was 'the vicious among the precious.' Conversely, when Rāvaṇa was in his palace, Hanumān's entry made him 'the precious among the vicious.' Vibhīṣaṇa, younger brother of Rāvaṇa, was also like a rose among the thorns. At Hastinapura, the vicious circle of the Kaurava brothers included Bhīṣma, Drōṇa and Vidura, the precious among the vicious. Conversely, the precious circle comprising Lord Kṛṣṇa and the Pāṇḍavas included Drupada, whose sole preoccupation was how to kill Drōṇa.

Being in the presence of a divine being is certainly a great blessing, but what one is thinking in that presence is equally important. Drupada was in the divine presence of Kṛṣṇa and the Pāṇḍavas, but his heart was filled with hatred, and thus he could not benefit from the Lord's divine presence. The gatekeepers of Vaikuṇṭha, brothers Jaya and Vijaya, became very egoistic and did not allow the four great sages to enter, and were thus cursed to be born as rākṣasas on earth.

Nāmadēv became proud because Śrī Kṛṣṇa would come to play with him. One day, Saint Jñānēśvar, his elder brother Nivṛttināth, younger brother Sōpān, and younger sister Muktābāī visited the Viṭhala temple. Usually, the devotees would touch Nāmadēv's feet in reverence. Jñanēśvar and his siblings did not, and this annoyed Nāmadēv. Jñānēśvar then set up a situation to remove Nāmadēv's ego.

During a gathering of mahātmās, Jñānēśvar asked Gora the potter, who was considered the most spiritually evolved, to tap the heads of the mahātmās to determine if they were fully 'baked' (spiritually mature). This is what potters do to find out if their pots are properly backed—they tap the pots. Gora did so, and then declared that all were fully baked except Nāmadēv.

Humiliated, Nāmadēv complained to Śrī Kṛṣṇa. The Lord said, "What Gora said is true. You are immature because you see Me only in this form, whereas Gora sees Me everywhere, in all forms. Go to Auṇḍhya Nāgnāth village, and there, you will find your Guru, Viśōbā Khēcar, who will give you true knowledge about Me!"

When Nāmadēv went to the Śiva temple, he saw an old man lying down with his feet placed on a Śiva Linga.[19] Outraged by this blasphemy, Nāmadēv shouted, "Old man, how dare you place your feet on the Śiva Linga? Remove them!"

Viśōbā Khēcar replied, "I am old and weak. Please remove my feet from the linga and place it somewhere else." Nāmadēv did

---

19 Literally, "mark of Śiva." The most prevalent icon of Lord Śiva, found in most Śiva temples. It is an elliptical form usually set on a circular base.

so, but to his surprise, another linga emerged from the ground to support Viśōbā's feet. Wherever Nāmadēv moved Viśōbā's feet, he was unable to keep them on the ground because a linga would appear to support the old man's feet. Realizing that this old man was the Guru whom Kṛṣṇa had indicated, Nāmadēv asked for forgiveness. He surrendered to his Guru, and in no time at all, Nāmadēv enjoyed the universal vision of Lord Kṛṣṇa.

After many years, when Nāmadēv was about to pass away, devotees asked him where they should inter his body. With joyful tears, Nāmadēv said, "Place my body beneath the steps leading to Lord Viṭhala in the temple. May the feet of His beloved devotees touch my head and sanctify me!"

Let us pray to Amma to make us like Saint Nāmadēv. The closer we are to Amma, the more humble we become, if we have the right attitude. This is real *satsang.*[20] Amma is like fire, and we, like wet wood. When wet wood is kept near fire, it soon dries and then catches fire. Similarly, the closer we are to Amma, the more we gain divine qualities like humility, compassion and patience.

For many years, Amma asked me to conduct Vēdānta classes for āśram residents. I felt that there were many senior swāmis who were more knowledgeable than I. Similarly, for many years, I used to play the harmonium for Amma during Her bhajans. Years ago, during the recording of '*Bhōlānathā Rē*,' I noticed

---

20 Being in communion with the Supreme Truth. Also being in the company of mahātmās, studying scriptures, listening to a spiritual talk or discussion, and participating in spiritual practices in a group setting.

how rapidly and beautifully the harmonium player was playing the musical interlude. I could never have played that way! I thought, "I am not an accomplished harmonium player, and yet Amma has made me one of Her instrumentalists!" May those who are always around Amma remain humble. The moment I think, "I am Amma's harmonium player. I am someone special," I debase myself by egoism. When I used to play the harmonium for Amma, if any stray thought came to mind during the bhajans, Amma would use Her stick to tap my hand or head, thus reminding me to stay focused on God. Being close to Amma means being mentally close to Her. Some devotees ritually circumambulate the hall while Amma is giving darśan, but they are constantly talking. The body goes round the hall, but the mind is elsewhere!

'*Manasā ēva idam āptavyam*' – 'This (Truth) has to be attained by the mind alone," declares the *Kaṭhōpaniṣad* (2.4.11). One may visit a temple every day, or go for pilgrimages every month, but if one's mind is not dwelling on the Lord, one attains little. Someone told me, "Swāmiji, I have chanted the *Gāyatrī* mantra[21] 50 *lākh* (five million) times!" Very good, but one should never be proud of it! With every repetition of the mantra, may the mind become humbler and humbler. Amma says, "I can tolerate anything in this world, but not the ego!" Egoism takes us away from the Precious One. The pure mind, constantly thinking of God, merges into Him.

---

21 Vēdic mantra that invokes Sāvitrī, a solar deity.

People who work in small groups, whether in their offices or other organizations, can become stuck with or attached to these small groups. In spiritual life, such attachment can hinder growth. Some aspirants refuse to emerge from their small circle; they do not permit anyone to enter it either! Let us not forget that a small pond with stagnant water becomes a breeding place for frogs and mosquitoes! We should instead strive to be like the vast and sacred Mānasarōvar Lake. By being inclusive and respectful of others' contributions, we become more expansive.

Selfish leaders try to make their communities air-tight compartments, i.e. like vicious circles, whereas spiritual leaders like Amma embrace everyone. Modern youth are often caught in vicious circles. Amma transforms them by making them aware of the divinity within. She helps them understand the difference between the delicious and the nutritious so that, gradually, they give up the delicious and choose the nutritious. As Voltaire, French writer, humanist and rationalist, said about God, Amma's real circle "is a circle whose centre is everywhere and circumference nowhere!"

SPIRITUAL WORK

Living Master

In a previous incarnation, the Buddha had been a king. Even then, His spiritual leanings were so acute that he decided to renounce the kingdom and embrace sanyāsa. His wife, a woman of breathtaking beauty, wanted to follow him to the forests. At first, the king refused, saying that she would not be able to adapt to the harsh jungle environment. But the queen was determined. She shaved her head and donned the simple robes of a monastic. Seeing this, the king relented. The couple traveled far away from the kingdom and went deep into the heart of a forest. There, they led an austere life, practicing strict spiritual disciplines.

One day, a king from a neighboring kingdom came by on horseback. He spotted the couple and was attracted by the beauty of the woman. Overcome by desire, he resolved to take her away. But doubts about the man next to her made him hesitate: what if he was a mahātmā with great powers? He decided to find out more about the man.

He stepped up and boldly announced his intention to the king-turned-monk. The latter, without showing any sign of perturbation, said, "I will not allow my enemy to overcome me."

The king did not understand the import of this remark. All the same, he ordered his soldiers to carry the woman forcibly and place her on his horse. Even then, the monk did not react in any way. The king asked, "Aren't you going to try and save your wife?"

"I will not allow my enemy to overcome me."

Puzzled, the king asked the monk what he meant. The monk replied, "When your soldiers were carrying my wife away, I was boiling with rage within. But I did not allow that negative emotion to overcome me. Negative emotions, thoughts and feelings are our real enemies. One who has control over them is truly powerful."

The king realized that he was indeed in the presence of a mahātmā. He prostrated before the monk and begged forgiveness for his rash and impulsive behavior. He then humbly offered the services of a few of his soldiers so that they could protect the monk's wife from further danger.

The greatness of individuals like the monk stems from their total control over their own minds, and not control of other people. A piece of advice that Amma often gives comes to mind: "Children, we should have the remote controls of our minds in our hands." She also compares the mind to a vehicle; it needs good brakes, or else, it runs the risk of collision. One whose mind is equipped with good brakes or who holds the mind's remote control enjoys uninterrupted peace, no matter what the external situation. For most of us, the ideal of such self-control is Amma.

Perhaps, this was why, when Amma asked, "What is the way to remain peaceful whether one is in a crowd or alone?" one of Her American children spontaneously replied, "By seeing everything as Amma; You accept everything and negate nothing!"

He pronounced "Amma" with the first vowel lengthened – "*Āma*." In Malayalam, '*āma*' means 'tortoise.' This association triggered off a new chain of thoughts in my mind. I remembered a mantra in the *Laḷitā Sahasranāma* (1,000 names of the Divine Mother): "*Ōm kūrma priṣṭha jayiṣṇu prapadānvitāyai namaḥ*" – "Salutations to Her, whose feet have insteps that rival the back of a tortoise in smoothness and beauty" (43). Amma's hallowed feet are a perfect actualization of this description. According to the scriptures, such a feature represents beauty.

But what does it really mean to have feet that resemble the carapace of a tortoise? For the ancient sages of India, the tortoise was a symbol of self-control, that is, withdrawal of one's senses from the external world:

1. At the slightest hint of danger, the tortoise withdraws its head and four legs into its hard shell, which serves as a protective armor. Similarly, a sādhak must learn to withdraw the five sense organs whenever there is a danger of the senses disturbing our inner poise. By thus calming the mind, we can make it more one-pointed in concentration, and more detached from the mundane world. The mental purity that follows accelerates one's spiritual progress and confers material benefits.

This principle is reflected in the *dīpasthambham*, the towering structure located in front of Hindu temples. The multi-tiered structure rests on the back of a figure of a tortoise. When the wicks on all the tiers are lit, the dīpasthambham turns into a dazzling pillar of light suggestive of spiritual splendor. It is symbolic of the glory and illumination that one attains after gaining self-control.

This victory is further indicated by the figure on top of the dīpastambham: a bull in a Śiva temple, a lion in a Durgā temple, and an eagle in a Viṣṇu temple. Like these animals, which are blessed to be carriers of the divine spirit, our lives will become divinely blessed if we gain self-control.

This idea is expressed in the *Bhagavad* Gītā too. Lord Kṛṣṇa says:

> *yadā samharate cāyam kūrmongānīva sarvaśaḥ*
> *indriyāṇindriyārthebhyastasya prajñā pratiṣṭhitā (2.58)*
>
> The yōgi who withdraws his sense organs from sense objects, just as the tortoise withdraws all its limbs, is rooted in divine wisdom.

2. Try lifting a tortoise that is moving in a particular direction and setting it down in another: it will turn and continue moving in the original direction; we will never be able to change its course. In the same way, a sādhak must always be goal-oriented—that is, God-oriented—despite all the challenges that confront him or her.

3. A tortoise is said to be slow and steady. Like the tortoise, the seeker must strive to be consistent in his or her sādhana so as to make progress steadily to ultimate liberation.

4. The tortoise is amphibious, i.e. it can live both on land and in water. Similarly, a sādhak must stay afloat in the waters of worldly life until he or she reaches the land of the Supreme. This means not letting the world and its siren calls mislead and take us away from our spiritual goal.

5. The female tortoise lays its eggs on the seashore but hatches them while in the ocean by the sheer power of constantly thinking about it. Similarly, though swimming in the ocean of worldly life, by constantly dwelling on God, a devotee awakens to divine awareness.

These are the few lessons that, by Amma's grace, I have learned from the humble tortoise.

The humble tortoise is elevated to the status of the divine in the *Bhāgavatam*, which chronicles the various incarnations of Lord Viṣṇu. In His incarnation as tortoise, referred to as the *kūrma avatār*, this divine tortoise supported the Mandāra Mountain, which the gods and demons used as churning rod to obtain *amṛta* (nectar of immortality). This signifies how all activity ought to be founded on self-control. Only a selfless person with self-control can succeed in spiritual life.

When we bow down and touch Amma's divine feet, let us pray to Her to bless us with purity and concentration of mind and make it a fit vehicle so that we may be able to proceed towards prosperity, peace, happiness and freedom.

From Hollowness to Holiness and Back

"Every soul is potentially divine," said a saint from recent times. The scriptures hold that when a person realizes the impermanence of worldly life, he or she approaches a Guru and in due course attains knowledge of the Self.

Ignorance is pardonable, but not ignorance of one's ignorance. The Guru helps the disciple or devotee realize that worldly achievements are, in the final analysis, no achievements after all. That person then becomes conscious of his or her hollowness. One could well prefix his or her name with 'H.H.' – 'His/Her Hollowness!'

At this stage, the Guru prescribes spiritual practices like mantra chanting and meditation. Eventually, the disciple's mind becomes pure, and he or she becomes fit for the honorific 'H.H.' – 'His/Her Holiness.'

While the chanting of mantras and meditation undoubtedly purifies a person, it is possible that the practitioner of these spiritual practices may, if not alert, become proud of his or her austerities. Viśvāmitra, a famous sage, could create a second heaven by the power of his tapas, but he was still caught in the grip of his ego.

The aim of performing austerities is to remove the ego. This is possible only with the help of a Guru who shatters the disciple's imagined aura of holiness. Thus, the disciple becomes hollow again. This time though, the hollowness is positive, arising from the understanding that the Supreme Being alone is real and the 'I,' only an appearance.

How can one be egoistic, knowing that it is the Supreme Being's presence in one's body that is behind all the different powers like intelligence and strength that one possesses? This hollowness enables the disciple to become like a flute in the hands of Lord Kṛṣṇa. He produces divine music through it. Such a disciple has realized his or her oneness with the whole universe, and may be hailed 'His/Her Wholeness.'

Conversely, how can one suffer from an inferiority complex knowing that the Supreme Being is close to oneself, within oneself, and enlivening and energizing every cell in oneself?

Amma removes both the negative feelings of "Oh, I am good for nothing!" (hollowness) and the egoistic one of "Oh, I am very pure, having performed so much austerity!" ('holiness'), and makes each one of us 'His/Her Wholeness.'

A.B.C. to I.P.S.

When I was young, I saw a film about a tribal woman going to the city for the first time. There, she saw a traffic policeman standing at the road junction and controlling the traffic with grandiose gestures. Simpleton that she was, the tribal woman was awed by the sight of the policeman and his seemingly grand powers. As she stood staring at him, she made a resolution: "When my son grows up, he will also become a traffic policeman!"

Everyone watching the movie burst into laughter at her simplicity and naïvete. Among the audience, there were parents with children. They, too, had hopes and aspirations for their children. Were those hopes and aspirations just as laughable?

Among Hindus, a major milestone is the *Akṣarabhyāsa*, a ceremony in which a child is initiated into learning. The word '*Akṣara*' has two meanings: the first is alphabet, and the second is Imperishable. When the Guru initiates us into learning, She hopes that through the alphabet, we will eventually attain the Imperishable, the Supreme.

In fact, Amma and the other mahātmās declare, "*Tat tvam asi*" ("That you are"). At present, we might aspire to become someone like Bill Gates. However, when we have attained That, we will see no difference between a billionaire CEO and the traffic policeman with his grandiose gestures.

There is nothing wrong with aspirations or ambitions. But let us aim well and high. Among the police, there is the SP (Superinendent of Police). In spiritual life, this is the ***Sat Puruṣa***, one who thinks only of the welfare of others. And then, there is the ***IPS*** (Indian Police Service), which, in spirituality, corresponds to the ***Infinite Parāśaktī Service***. The qualifications to entering the ranks of the IPS are Innocence, Purity and Simplicity. In truth, we all belong to the IPS cadre. The highest rank is that of the ***DGP*** (Deputy General of Police)—in spirituality, this is the ***Divine Guide*** to ***Peace***. This position is held by none other than our beloved Amma.

A Satguru like Amma helps us use karma to elevate ourselves spiritually. She has liberated many from their slavish dependence on objects of enjoyment. These blessed souls discover a new joy in Amma's divine presence. Drug addicts become hug addicts. We know how to bathe our bodies only, but our mind also needs a daily bath. Amma's hug is a body-and-mind bath. It purifies, refreshes and energizes both.

If a bear hugged us or if a python coiled around us, we would be finished! But Amma's hug revitalizes us, bringing us in direct contact with divinity. Lord Rāma hugged Hanumān joyfully when Hanumān returned from Lanka after discovering Sītā's whereabouts and giving Rāvaṇa a taste of Rāma's infinite might. When Kucēla (also known as Sudāma), Lord Kṛṣṇa's childhood friend, paid the Lord a visit in Dvāraka, Kṛṣṇa hugged Sudāma. For the first time in His life, His queens and courtiers saw tears in His eyes. In the *Rāmāyaṇa*, when the Rāvaṇa's army of *rakṣasas* (demons) appeared to be winning the war against Rāma's army of vānaras, Sage Agastya appeared and advised Lord Rāma to use the *mohana-astra*, a deluding weapon, on both the armies.

Owing to the spell of the astra, all the vanaras and rakshasas appeared as Lord Rāma. There were countless forms of Lord Rāma on the battlefield! The rakṣasas, seeing their sworn enemy around them, started attacking each other, and every one of them perished! When the vānaras saw their beloved Lord around them, they started hugging each other and falling at each other's feet!

Amma hugged the former Indian President Abdul Kalam as well as Narendra Modi and Vajpayee, the present and former Indian Prime Ministers respectively with great enthusiasm. She hugged Dattan, the leper, just as enthusiastically. This is because She beholds divinity in all beings.

In the *Rāmāyaṇa*, before the search for Sītā began, Hanumān and Sugrīva stood in front of Lord Rāma. Lord Rāma could have told Sugrīva, "You know what the pangs of separation from your wife feel like. I give you strength to go in search of Sītā!" But Lord Rāma sent Hanumān instead because the pang of separation Sītā was experiencing was not a wife's pain of separation from her husband, but the pain a devotee feels in being separated from Her Lord. Hanumān understood this pain, which is why Lord Rāma sent him.

In the *Bhāgavata Katha*, it is Sage Śukadēv, a *nitya-brahmacārī* (eternal celibate), who narrates the rāsa līla. What does a brahmacārī know about romance and love-making? Why did the Lord chose Śukadēv instead of Kāmadēv, the Indian Cupid, to narrate the rāsa līla? Because the union of Kṛṣṇa and the gōpīs was not a physical union but the union of *jīvātmas* (individuated souls) with the Paramātma, and Śukadēva had experienced that mystic union.

We hear people say, "I *fell* in love..." But in true love, there can be no fall. One can fall in lust, passion, infatuation or attachment, but one *rises* in true love!

Amma's hug unites Parāśaktī with alpaśaktīs, Her children. It is **H**uman **U**nity with **G**od. In Her hug, we experience **H**umanity's **U**ltimate **G**oal.

The millions who come to see Amma in Amṛtapuri and other places experience divine love, compassion as well as a new strength and vitality in Her love. They sit together with silent, blissful tears and a sense of fulfilment. In Amma's divine presence, they become a **H**armonious **U**niversal **G**athering. Amma is the **A**lmighty's **M**anifestation as **M**other of **A**ll.

Lord Yama, the God of Death, carries a noose or rope ('*pāśa*' in Sānskṛt) with which he yanks the jīvātma out of the body. Goddess Durgā also has a pāśa. The *Durgā Kavacam* proclaims, "*Paraśum pāśam eva ca.*" Among the many weapons She holds in Her eight are the *paraśu* (ax) and pāśa. With the ax, She severs all attachments and bondages. She then binds us to Her with the rope of motherly love. With every attachment, we climb down the ladder or fall into bondage. However, attachment to the Guru or God takes one up the same ladder to Freedom, Peace and Infinite Joy.

Amma says that Her hug is not a union of two bodies but of two hearts. It denotes a total acceptance of the other, seeing him or her as a form of God. Amma sees all forms as Her own and accepts them. She is in the highest state. I remember a verse on Śukadēv, with which the *Bhāgavatam* begins:

> *yam pravajantam anupētam apēta kṛtyam*
> *dvaipāyana viraḥ katara ājuhava*
> *putrēti tanmayatayā taravōSvinēdus*
> *tvam sarvabhūta hṛdayam munim ānatōsmi*
>
> I offer my respectful obeisance to the great sage, who can enter everyone's heart and whom his father, Vyāsa, called 'my son' while the son was leaving to assume a life of renunciation without undergoing the sacred thread or other ceremonies observed by the higher castes. The trees responded to the fearful father, who was feeling the separation from the son. (*Śrīmad Bhāgavatam*, 1.2.2)

Śukadēv was called 'anupētam,' i.e. one who had not undergone *upanayana* ceremony, which qualifies one for various spiritual practices that ultimately leads to liberation. He was also called 'apēta kṛtyam,' i.e. one who is above the moral regulations (*yamas, niyamas, dharma,* etc.) by which human beings in general are expected to abide. Śukadēv was already in the highest state when born. He is called 'sarvabhūta hṛdayam.' As soon as he was born, he walked away to take sanyāsa, the formal vows of renunciation. When his father Sage Vyāsa called out to him, "O Śuka!" all the trees responded in unison, "Yes, father!" It showed that Śukadēv had become identified with all beings in this universe, and therefore none of the ethical norms could bind him.

Amma is also in this state—or we could say, above it. At the end of the *Mahābhārata*, when the infant Parīkṣit in Uttarā's womb was killed by the divine weapon of Aśvatthāma, Vyāsa declared that if a nitya-brahmacārī touched the baby, he would come back to life. Even Śukadēv hesitated to touch the baby. But Lord Kṛṣṇa touched the baby, which came back to life. Amma is like Kṛṣṇa; none of Her actions can sully or bind Her. In any case, how can human minds ever correctly gauge the actions of mahātmās?

Mahātmās like Amma manifest all the virtues in their purest forms. Her smile is the purest form of smile, and Her patience, the purest form of patience. There is blazing purity even in Her anger! In contrast, in human beings, even love is adulterated. Recently, I heard about a youngster who consumed poison but fortunately did not die because the poison was adulterated!

When Śrī Rāma shot the fatal arrow at Rāvaṇa, He had only love in His heart. When Śrī Kṛṣṇa unleashed the *Sudarśana Cakra*[22] at Śiśupāla, He had only love in His heart! Both Rāvaṇa and Śiśupāla attained salvation. All mahātmās are like surgeons, who might cause pain only to cure their patients.

Recently, someone asked me, "Who is the Vice-Chancellor of Amrita University?" I answered his question, and then an interesting thought came to my mind. I thought of the many well-educated devotees who had left their well-paying jobs and comfortable lives in India or abroad to join Amma's āśram. They are 'wise chance-llors,' who had wisely seized the precious chance

---

22 A spinning, disk-like weapon; associated with Lord Viṣṇu.

of living with a mahātmā. And then there were those who, unable to stop their bad habits, took refuge in Amma; thereafter, their vices were 'cancelled,' so to say. They are the 'vice cancellers.' And so, Amṛtapuri has many Vice-Chancellors. The reason behind this is Amma's Hug, the embrace that draws people away from selfishness to the spiritual path.

Real Longing

In North India, there was a virtuous king named Śivāji. One day, while strolling in his mango grove, a stone suddenly came flying from somewhere and hit his head. His bodyguards ran off at once in all directions. Soon, they arrested an elderly woman. They took her to the king and told him that it was she who had thrown the stone. When asked why she had done so, the old woman said, "I'm very sorry, Your Majesty. There hasn't been anything to eat in my house for many days, and my son is dying of hunger. So, I went in search of food. When I saw some mangoes, I took a stone and threw it at one of the mango trees to make the mangoes fall down. Unfortunately, that stone landed on your head. Please forgive me."

After thinking for some time, the king asked, "What did you get?"

"When the stone hit the tree, three ripe mangoes fell down," the woman replied.

Śivāji said, "If a mere tree is kind enough to give three mangoes after being injured, I, as a human being, must give you something more."

He then had a sumptuous feast prepared for the mother and son. He also secured employment for the young man and enough wealth for the family so that they would never be in want anymore.

This human body is given to us for some purpose. The question is, how to use it properly? Of what use is a beautiful wristwatch studded with precious gems, if it does not show the right time? It can be compared to a man who is not righteous. One does not say, "It's hot fire." If it is fire, it will be hot; heat is the very nature of fire. Likewise, we need not say, "He is a righteous man." If he is a true man, he will be righteous. Otherwise, he will be like an animal.

Some years ago, a devotee from Delhi donated a car to Amma. The car had to be taken to Amṛtapuri, a journey of about seven days by road. What would be the attitude of the brahmacārī driving the car? The car does not belong to him, but to Amma. Therefore, he has to be very careful. To a certain extent, he has some freedom. For example, if the tire is punctured, he can replace it himself; he need not call Amma and tell Her about it. However, suppose he does not like the color of the car and wants to change it. He first has to ask Amma for permission to do so.

In the same way, our body is a vehicle given to us by God. Only He has the right to change it. We must use our God-given discretion for other matters, such as how much we can eat. But as this body belongs to God, we must not torture it.

The Buddha used to do intense tapas. Once, he remained seated in meditation without eating and drinking anything for many days. His body became lean and weak. One day, a music teacher and his student came and sat down near the Buddha. They had a *vīṇā*[23] with them, and the teacher started explaining how to tune the instrument. He said, "If you tighten the strings

23 Indian stringed instrument

too much, they will break. But if they are slack, no music will come from them."

The Buddha, who was listening, understood the message: avoid extremes. Too much of tapas breaks the strings of the mind, but indulging in pleasure brings about one's spiritual downfall. From that day onwards, the Buddha followed the middle path and attained Self-realization within a short time.

Many devotees ask Amma, "How can we know whether we are progressing on the spiritual path?"

Amma said, "If you feel compassion towards others arising in your heart, then you can be sure that you are progressing. But if, even after many years of spiritual practice, you don't feel any compassion for living beings, then be sure that you haven't progressed at all!"

There was a sādhak staying in a small hut at the foot of a mountain. He took a firm vow that he would not eat or drink anything from sunrise to sunset. After some time, he saw a beautiful star on the Eastern horizon and heard a voice say that it was a symbol of his noble austerities.

One day, as he walked across the mountain, a small boy accompanied him. After some time, it became very hot, and the two became extremely thirsty. When they passed a little stream, the sādhak gave the boy a small vessel and told him to fill it with water. The boy filled it with water, and offered it to the sādhak, who declined because of his vow. Seeing this, the boy said that, in that case, he, too, would not drink.

The sādhak was in a dilemma. He did not want to break his vow, but he also did not want the boy to suffer because of him. He finally thought, "This boy is extremely tired and thirsty. Let me break my fast for his sake and drink a little water." After he had taken one sip, the boy immediately started drinking.

The man was a little unhappy as he had broken his vow. Hesitatingly, he looked at the Eastern horizon to see what had happened to the star. To his surprise, there were two beautiful stars to be seen now.

It was a sign that he was progressing. Through his austerities, he was able to purify his mind, and as a result, compassion blossomed in his heart. That compassion, which is love without attachment, is the sign of progress.

The so-called love that human beings have for each other is nothing but attachment. Usually, the love we feel towards a person is directly proportional to what we get from him or her. The more we get from someone, the more we 'love' him or her. Conversely, the less we get, the less we 'love.' Attachment is bondage, but true love, in which there is no expectation of return, is freedom.

Actually, we cannot really offer anything to Amma, because nothing belongs to us, not even the body. So how can we speak of offering anything? Our only creation is the mind. And that is what we can offer Amma.

The mind can be compared to a forest. One tree does not make a forest, which is a dense and large cluster of trees. In the same way, the mind is a flow of thoughts. The question arises: how to control this cascade? How to discipline the mind?

The *Bhagavad Gītā* uses the analogy of the chariot. The five horses yoked to it signify the five sense organs; the reins, the different thoughts of the mind; the charioteer, the discriminative intellect; and the chariot, the human body. The horses are controlled by the reins, which are controlled by the charioteer. If we control the horses properly, they will take us to our destination. Likewise, if the senses are under our control, then we will reach our goal. However, if the reins are let loose and the horses go wild, they will take us wherever they want.

A landlord told his tenant, a young man, to vacate the apartment within a week. At first, he did not know what to do. Suddenly, he remembered his old friend, James. He thought, "Ah, yes! I'm sure James will help me. He has his own apartment. He can accommodate me." After some time, another thought arose in his mind, "What if he doesn't want me to stay there?" He felt a little peeved at the idea, and thought, "Why not? After all, I helped him get his present job. Well, let me go and ask him." A few minutes later, he started thinking again, "Suppose James doesn't accommodate me. What will I do?" Again, he got angry. "Has he forgotten that it was I who got him the apartment? Many years ago, I even saved him from drowning. He *should* accommodate me!"

By now, he was very angry. He rushed to James's house and rang the bell furiously. It was already past midnight. James opened the door, and said, "What a surprise! What brings you here at this late hour? Please come in."

The man shouted, "No! I'm not coming in! Even if you invite me to stay at your house, I'm not going to set foot in it! Good bye!"

This is undisciplined thinking. It is hell. Heaven and hell are within us. If we know how to discipline our mind, we will be peaceful—we will enjoy heaven. If our thinking is undisciplined, then we experience hell.

King Janaka, Sītā's father, had an intense longing for Self-realization. He asked all the sages he met, "Can you give me Self-realization?" But no one could fulfill his desire.

One day, a young sage named Aṣṭavakra, who was established in the Supreme Consciousness, came to the king and said, "I will give you what you want, but you have to do what I say. It implies total surrender." The king, who was very anxious to attain the ultimate goal of human life, promptly accepted this condition. Aṣṭavakra said, "First, you must surrender everything to me."

"Surrendered," said the king.

"Very good! Now, get down from the throne, and sit where the footwear is kept."

Without a moment's hesitation, Janaka sat there, using his sandals as *āsana* (seat).

The sage said, "Now, not only your kingdom and body, your mind also belongs to me. Therefore, don't think anything without my permission. Stop thinking!"

The king had so much self-control and such a strong desire to know the truth that his mind became completely still and he attained God-realization.

A yōgi's mind goes wherever he or she wants it to go, whereas in most of our cases, we go wherever the mind takes us. A lot of disciplining is necessary to gain mental control. We can start by concentrating the mind on the form of our *iṣṭa-dēvatā* (preferred form of divinity). We can choose any form we like. All the different steps in *pūjā* (ritualistic worship) help to fix the mind on the iṣṭa dēvatā and to forget the outer world.

A child first rides a tricycle. When he has learned how to balance, he can ride a bicycle. When he becomes even more accomplished, he might even be able to ride a unicycle. In the same way, in the beginning stages of spiritual life, we need to use the three wheels of thought, speech and action. In pūjā, one uses the mind, words and body to gain concentration. When we have progressed, we may stop doing the pūjā externally, and continue doing it with words (e.g. *mantra japa*, i.e. repeated chanting of the mantra) and the mind. Finally, at an advanced stage, we may even stop worship using words, and use only the mind to remember God.

When we are very tired, we think only of sleep. Actually, it is not just a thought but a powerful feeling, too. This powerful thought-feeling effortlessly removes every other thought and drags one to the bedroom to sleep. This is called *bhāvana*. Similarly, when the longing for God becomes intense, the heart and the head work together. When there is such intensity, nothing else matters. In that state, we surrender ourselves completely to that hitherto unknown peace and bliss, sit quietly and wait patiently to be lifted into the highest state by the Guru.

With a Paramahamsini

A few months after I joined Amma's āśram in 1986, I asked Her, "Amma, please give me enlightenment."

Amma smiled and asked me, "What will happen if 20,000 volts is passed through a 20-watt bulb?"

"The bulb will blow!" I replied.

Amma smiled and said, "The same thing will happen to you also!"

Amma was teaching me that the body-mind vessel must have the purity and strength to withstand the impact of the Infinite manifesting in the heart. Even Narēn, who later became the world-famous Swāmi Vivēkānanda, became frightened when Śrī Rāmakṛṣṇa Paramahamsa gave him an experience of the Infinite by touching his heart.

Emperor Bhāgīratha performed tapas to bring the sacred Gangā River down to earth in order to cleanse the sins of his uncles who had perished as a result of Sage Kapila's curse. Mother Gangā said, "I am ready to descend to earth, but who will bear the weight and force of my descent?"

Bhāgīratha did tapas again and pleaded with Lord Śiva to receive Mother Gangā. The Lord did so, absorbing the Ganges in the matted locks on His head and then releasing Her as a thin stream. Enlightenment is like the descent of Gangā; if unmediated, we will be washed away. Like Śiva, the Guru bestows it on us in a way in which we can experience the infinite peace and joy within ourselves. For some, like the *avadhūtas*,[24] the powerful experience of enlightenment proves so overwhelming that they lose all control; they start jumping and dancing like madmen.

The Guru is like the sun, and the Vēdic scriptures, like the ocean. The sun draws up water from the ocean. The evaporated water forms clouds that eventually burst, causing rain to fall. Similarly, the Guru dispenses the ocean of Vēdic wisdom to us through the gentle shower of spiritual teachings. We know how simple Amma's teachings are.

Yōgic exercises make the body-mind vessel strong, pure and receptive to experience God. Amma's āśrams and educational institutions celebrate International Yōga Day on June 21st. Recently, while watching school children perform yōga āsanas, I thought, "Performing yōga āsanas is easy for them because their bodies are young and flexible. But is it easy for them to follow the yōgic diet?" A yōgic diet is as important as the yōga āsanas. Yōga is not for heavy consumers of oily and spicy foods.

For those who wish to control their diet but find it difficult, they can take heart in this: that constantly chanting the mantra Amma has given us gives us strength to control our tongue and other organs.

Kṛṣṇa and His elder brother Balarām were walking in the streets of Mathura when they saw a hunchback. Kṛṣṇa went up to her, called her "Sundarī" (meaning "Beautiful one"), pressed His divine feet on hers and, with His hands, lifted her chin. The

---

24 An enlightened person whose behavior transcends social norms.

woman's backbone straightened, and her hunch disappeared. She was transformed into a beautiful woman. The spiritual masters say that Yōga is not twisting the body but straightening the mind. Divine doctors like Kṛṣṇa and Amma straighten not only our bodies but our minds as well.

Lord Kṛṣṇa was 82 years old and Arjuna, 80, when they fought the Mahābhārata War in Kurukṣetra. Today, anyone over 65 is considered old, but in those days, one could be a warrior even in one's 80s!

Leo Tolstoy, the famous Russian writer, tells an interesting story. One morning, a farmer found a wheat grain that was as big as an egg and as shiny as gold. He took it to the king and showed it to him. Surprised, the king called all the farmers in his kingdom, showed them the grain, and asked if any one of them had seen such a variety. Nobody had, but the eldest farmer, who was very old and who could hardly walk, said, "Let me bring my father!"

When the old farmer's father came, everyone was surprised to see that he looked much healthier and younger than his son. The father looked at the grain and said, "No, I've never seen a grain of this size and quality, but let me bring my father!"

The grandfather was even younger, healthier and stronger looking than his son and grandson! He looked at the grain and said, "O king, during my youth, we *did* have grains of this size. Those were times when everyone loved one another. Jealousy and hatred were unknown. Nobody owned any land. When one needed grain, one would select a vacant plot, sow seeds, reap the harvest, take only what one needed for a year, and then give the remaining grains to the needy! That is why nature blessed us with such big grains and gave us long life with health and youthfulness!"

The story reminds us of Amma's teachings on living in harmony with nature and on living a life of giving and sharing.

Yōga is union with God. Every one of the 18 chapters in the *Bhagavad Gītā* is called yōga. The first chapter is called *'Arjuna Viṣāda Yōga,'* the Yōga of Arjuna's Despondency. Sorrow takes him closer to God. The second chapter is *Jñāna Yōga* (the Yōga of Knowledge), the third, *Karma Yōga* (the Yōga of Action), and so on and so forth. All the chapters contain techniques, teachings and advice that enable us to merge gradually with God.

The *Bhagavad Gītā* teaches us many things about yōga:

> *yōgaḥ karmasu kauśalam*
>
> Yōga is skill in action. (2.50)
>
> *samatvam yōga ucyate*
>
> Evenness of mind is yōga. (2.48)

Yōga āsanas, which the ancient ṛṣis bequeathed to all of humanity, help us become fully conscious of our bodies, their functions and their movements. Yōga then makes us aware of our emotions and thoughts, and finally takes us beyond the mental level to the spiritual level, wherein we come face to face with pure awareness, which is our real nature. Traditional dances such as *Bhāratanatyam* and traditional martial arts like *kaḷari payaṭṭu* also teach us to transcend body consciousness. It was this transcendental awareness that Lord Kṛṣṇa alluded to when He said,

> *na hanyatē hanyamānē śarirē*
>
> One is not killed even when the body is destroyed. (*Bhagavad Gītā*, 2.20)

Once, a group of Buddhist itinerant monks entered a tea shop. The owner himself served them tea in beautiful cups. As all the monks looked alike, the owner could not identify the Guru. But the owner was a wise man. He carefully watched as the monks silently drank from the cups. He noticed that one person drank his tea differently from the others. He lifted his cup gracefully with total awareness, as if it were a new-born baby. And he sipped the tea as if he were lovingly kissing the baby. He seemed to be aware even of the batting of his eyelids and his breathing. Realizing that he was the Guru, the proprietor of the tea shop walked up to him and prostrated.

I have seen youngsters sit and stand during mass drills. Their sitting is a crash landing, and they stand as if jumping up from a hot stove! Despite their energy, they lack awareness.

Yōga helps us go beyond death. Death is only for the body and for those who identify with the body. Yama, the Lord of Death, rides on a buffalo, which is the very embodiment of *tamas*—laziness, lethargy and ignorance. The image of Yama on a buffalo signifies that death seizes the ignorant; it cannot touch those who know that they are not the body but pure consciousness.

All beings are a mixture of consciousness and matter. Matter comes in different forms, but consciousness is one; it is formless. A thousand mud pots of different sizes have the same space in each one of them. Matter is like the pots, and consciousness, like space. Mahātmās can distinguish consciousness from matter, and being able to see beyond all differences, they accept every living being in this universe.

In Indian mythology, the swan ('*hamsa*' in Sanskrit) is celebrated for its rare ability to separate milk from a solution of milk and water. The most spiritually evolved saints are honored with the epithet '*Paramahamsa*,'[25] Supreme Swan, for their natural ability to see the one Self in all beings, regardless of the form it assumes. Amma is a Paramahamsinī. Her ability to love one and all unconditionally reveals Her *sama-dṛṣṭi*, equal vision. Amma has also said that She sees the Self in one and all, as if She were looking into a mirror.

Amma sings the following bhajan, which reveals, through negation, our true identity:

> *manō buddhi ahankāra cittāni nāham*
> *cidānanda rūpaḥ śivōham śivōham*
>
> I am not mind, intellect, ego or memory
> I am the Pure Awareness-Bliss, I am Śiva! I am Śiva!

Let us pray to Amma to take us to that state of realization.

25 The feminine equivalent is 'paramhamsinī.'

"Enlightenment? Peanuts for Me!"

During a lunch stop on the North Indian tour in 2010, Amma made a profound statement: "Enlightenment is like peanuts for me. I give glory to the person who performs selfless actions with full devotion, faith and surrender."

Enlightenment is knowing oneself as infinite consciousness, existence and bliss. It is realizing and experiencing that the one Supreme Being alone appears as the countless forms in the universe.

Most of us have only individuated body-and-mind consciousness. I don't know what you are thinking; you don't know what is in my mind either. But Amma who has risen above the body and the mind knows everything in the minds of all human beings, including their past, present and future.

During the earlier days in the āśram, Amma used to come with a handful of pebbles for meditation. She would know at once if a stray thought arose in the mind of anyone, and she would throw a stone at that person to bring that person's mind back to the object of her meditation.

The consummation of meditation is Liberation, wherein one experiences infinite bliss. All the scriptures and Gurus declare that this is the goal of human life, attaining which, one is never again subject to birth and death. The wise advise us not to run after material objects and sensual pleasures because they give us no permanent joy. Even though we know this, very few want Enlightenment. We are steeped in ignorance. We are like those who are slumbering. Amma is the power who is awake. What can she do to wake us up? Just give us a gentle tap or shake, and say, "Son/Daughter, get up!" It is easy for Amma to do that. I think this is what she meant when she said, "Enlightenment is like peanuts for me."

Enlightenment is available to all, not just the wise, knowledgeable or rich. Amma says Enlightenment is not the monopoly of any individual; it is for all. Unfortunately, most people don't want it as they are busy running after impermanent objects. Only a few discriminating individuals seek the permanent. They are like light sleepers; just a gentle tap, and they wake up. Some others are more deeply sunk in slumber; they need to be shaken violently so that they can wake up. But some are so blindly attached to the world and its objects; they are like drunken men who have fallen unconscious—a gentle tap or even a violent slap will not do; one has to wait until the effect of the alcohol has worn off. The Guru has infinite patience. She waits.

The *Bhagavad Gītā* describes three types of individuals afflicted by ignorance and attachment. In the first type, there is very little impurity of mind. Their minds are like a flame covered by smoke; one puff, and the smoke goes away. Enlightenment is easy for them.

There is more impurity in the second type of person. His mind is like a mirror covered by dust. More effort is required to wipe the mirror clean. Enlightenment takes more time for them.

The third type of mind is very impure. Such a mind is like a baby in the womb; you have to wait for nine months before the baby is born. Similarly, minds that are too impure take a long time to become enlightened.

Remember what Amma said: "I give glory to the person who performs selfless actions with full devotion, faith and surrender." The minds of most people are impure. Doing selfless actions with devotion, faith and surrender is the only way to rid the mind of its impurities. Once the mind is sufficiently purified, one can sit in meditation and slowly discover Infinite Consciousness within. If someone with an impure mind tries to meditate, he will fall asleep and slip deeper into ignorance. There are people who do not want to perform any selfless service, but want to meditate. Such people are lazy. Amma's words are a warning to them. She glorifies the intelligent person who is aware of his impurities, who knows that selfless actions purify him and ultimately take him to Enlightenment through meditation.

Spare the Rod, Spoil the Child

Once, the steps leading to the shrine of a temple asked the idol, "We're stones, just like you. Yet devotees trample upon us and break coconuts on us, whereas they offer you milk and ghee and perform all other kinds of pūjās. Why is that?"

The idol replied, "To shape stones into rectangular steps isn't too difficult. You don't undergo much pain. But do you know how much pain I underwent when the sculptor was chiseling and molding me?"

A Guru is like a sculptor, and the disciple's mind like a shapeless stone. The Guru transforms the shapeless stone into a beautiful idol by Her teachings and disciplining. Students who learn martial-art forms like kaḷari, kung fu and karate undergo a lot of physical pain. Their masters and seniors hit them to make their limbs strong and hard as steel. In the same way, spiritual masters subject their disciples to severe tests, which make the disciples' minds strong enough to face the challenges of life. In Amṛtapuri, the first temple where Amma used to give Bhāva darśan is called 'kaḷari,' a place where disciples are trained to become strong.

There is much debate on whether it is right for parents to beat their children. In some Western countries, it is unlawful for parents to spank their children. My history teacher said that Roman fathers had the right even to kill their children; this is extreme. In Kēraḷa, there is an old saying—"*Aḍiyāl kuṭṭi paṭhikkum,*" i.e. a child will learn only through beatings. Another group argues against this, saying *"Aḍiyāl kuṭṭi paṭṭiyākum,"* i.e. through beatings, a child becomes like a dog, totally insecure and lacking in self-confidence.

A Guru like Amma follows the middle path. She first showers Her children with motherly love, which binds them to Her, then starts disciplining them like a sculptor fashioning shapeless stones into idols.

There is an ancient saying:

> *tāḍanē bahavō dōṣāḥ*
> *lālanē bahavō gunāḥ*
> *tasmāt putram ca siśyam ca*
> *tāḍayēt na tu lālayēt*
>
> There are many advantages in disciplining and many disadvantages in pampering one's children. Therefore, discipline your children and disciples. Do not pamper them.

There is a story of how a widowed queen trained her son. When enemies attacked her kingdom, she sent her army to fight them. Even the young prince was sent along. While the war was going on, a soldier came to the queen and told her, "The prince died in the battle. We saw him lying dead with a wound in his back."

Shocked, the queen replied, "I don't believe it. Let me see." She went to the battlefield, where she saw the prince lying dead with a wound on the chest, not on his back. Turning to the soldier, she said, "See that? This is my son. He would never have run away from the enemy, showing them his back!"

Amma is such a mother. We enjoy Her disciplining because the love She pours on us makes us realize that She is molding us. Just as a doctor knows the right dosage of medicine for patients of different ages, a Guru like Amma knows what is best for Her children and disciples.

There are three types of patients just as there are three types of disciples. A few keep quiet even when undergoing painful treatment because they know that it is for their own good. Some complain about the pain, but accept the treatment. Yet others not only refuse to be treated, they even criticize the doctor.

If the child is spoiled or pampered by his parents, then he may face resistance from his peers or society. He is likely to be selfish and a menace to both himself and others. A child who is disciplined at a young age grows up into a well-mannered adult. Such a person develops the resilience to deal with difficulties that life presents.

The Meditative and the Active

Some devotees ask, “What can I do for Amma?”

It is heartening to hear this question. Generally, people think only about what they can get instead of what they can give. The word ‘go-getter’ refers to a person who is smart enough to get whatever he wants, wherever he goes. In contrast, the question “What can I give?” comes from a more mature and evolved person.

“What should my sādhana be?” is another question devotees ask. The answer to this question must come directly from the Guru. The sādhana that Amma prescribes for Her children may vary from person to person. She knows which sādhana can purify a particular sādhak by removing his or her inherent negative tendencies and *prārabdha* (results of actions done in the past that will manifest in the present lifetime). To different people, Amma recommends meditation, *mantra japa* (repeated chanting of a mantra), *arcana* (chanting of a litany of sacred names), *bhajan* (singing of devotional songs), *sēva* (selfless service), and charitable activities.

Here is a piece of beautiful advice on what should be done by whom:

> *dvau ambhasi nivēṣṭavyau galē baddhvā dṛḍhām śilām*
> *dhanavantam adātāram daridram ca atapasvinam*
>
> There are two types of people who ought to be pushed in deep water with heavy stones tied to their body: one who

> does not donate in spite of being rich, and the other who does not work hard, though poor. (*Mahābhārata*, verse 5.33.65)

For the rich, doing charitable deeds is recommended as a spiritual practice, whereas for a poor person, tapas is recommended. What type of tapas one does depends on the type of mind and body one has. All types of sādhana are important, but the proportion varies from seeker to seeker. One can learn how much of each to do only from a Guru.

Devotees can be broadly divided into two: meditative and active. In the *Bhagavad Gītā*, Lord Kṛṣṇa tells Arjuna:

> *lokēऽsmin dvividhā niṣṭhā purā proktā mayānagha*
> *jñānayōgēna sānkhyānam karmayōgēna yōginām*
>
> In this world, there is a two-fold path, as I taught before: the path of knowledge for the meditative type, and the path of action for the active type. (3.3)

Note that Lord Kṛṣṇa says, "*dvividhā niṣṭhā,*" i.e. a two-fold path (singular), and not two paths (plural). This means that jñāna yōga and karma yōga are two stages of the same path. Karma yōga comes first, and it brings about purification, steadiness and concentration of mind. Then comes jñāna yōga, by which one realizes one's innate nature as divine consciousness.

Some wrongly regard the two as distinctive paths. Of these, some go straight to the *jñāna mārga* (path of knowledge) without first passing through the *karma mārga* (path of action). They make little or no progress because their minds have not been purified by karma. Others stick to karma, refusing to move on to the jñāna mārga. Such people sink deeper into bondage. The right approach takes one through karma yōga and then to jñāna yōga. Only one who has purified himself mentally through karma yōga can go deep into meditation. Only those who meditate deeply can perform actions efficiently. Therefore, karma yōga and jñāna yōga are complimentary.

The main sādhana for reaching the human goal, i.e. Self-realization, is *dhyāna* (meditation), which leads to jñāna, the realization of our real nature as divine consciousness. All other sādhanas, like mantra japa and arcana, are supporting sādhanas.

Generally, people give a lot of importance to human effort, and either ignore or give undue importance to divine grace. A true aspirant, however, realizes as she progresses in her spiritual life that divine grace alone takes one closer to the Goal, and that even effort is impossible without divine grace.

The sādhana that the Guru prescribes is like medicine and diet. When the doctor prescribes a particular regimen of medicine and diet, we stick to it. We must be just as particular, if not more, about following what the Guru says. Some devotees become upset, thinking that the Guru has given others more. This is caused by flawed thinking.

A few years ago, a devotee unhappily told me, "Swāmiji, Amma has not understood my capacity. She has given me very few responsibilities!" He wanted to be entrusted with more responsibilities. By Amma's grace, I somehow managed to convince him that Amma knows what is best for him.

Some complain, "My Guru has given me too much work. I'm not able to meditate like others, who get more time to do so!" This grievance is unfounded. Whatever the Guru has entrusted to the disciple is sādhana that will best expedite her spiritual growth.

In the early days of my āśram life, I had to conduct classes for āśram residents and feed the cows as well. If a disciple is allowed to choose her own sādhana, she is likely to reinforce her personal likes and dislikes, which lead to greater bondage. A wise disciple never says, "Guruji, I don't want this. I want only that!" Instead, she will say, "Guruji, whatever you choose for me is best for me!"

Every individual is a bundle of likes and dislikes. The moment one wakes up, one's likes and dislikes become active. "I prefer brand A of toothpaste to brand B. I like coffee; I don't like tea..." Likes and dislikes tie us down to mundane life. We also suffer in the presence of people whose likes and dislikes don't match and are more powerful than ours.

However, we are ready to sacrifice our individual likes and dislikes for the sake of those whom we love. For example, a woman may like tea whereas her husband may prefer coffee. In order to save his wife from the trouble of making both coffee and tea, the husband may say, "Tea will do for me."

Similarly, all of us love Amma. Giving up our individual likes and dislikes for Amma's sake is the best offering to Amma. Not that She gains anything from our doing so; when we go beyond our likes and dislikes, the shackles preventing us from soaring into the spiritual empyreans slowly break open.

Alternatively, we should cultivate likes and dislikes that can benefit the maximum number of people.

Generally, we find that people are addicted to some kind of noise all the time. They cannot tolerate silence and become very restless when made to remain in a silent place for a long time. They are dependent on sound. On the contrary, many spiritual seekers unconsciously become addicted to silence! Even the smallest noise disturbs them. This is another kind of dependence. The worldly person depends on noise for happiness whereas the meditator depends upon silence for experiencing joy. Both are dependent; both are in bondage.

A realized soul like Amma, however, depends neither on sound nor silence! Whether She is in a noisy place or a silent one, Amma is absolutely at peace. Such is the real Guru.

The *Dakṣinamūrti Stōtram* speaks about the Guru thus:

> *nidhayē sarva vidyānām biṣajē bhāva rogināṃ*
> *guravē sarva lōkānām dakṣinamūrtayē namaḥ*
>
> I bow down to Dakṣinmūrti, the abode of all learning, the Physician to all those afflicted with the disease of worldly existence, the Teacher of all. (4)

The Guru is described as "biṣajē bhāva rogināṃ"—the doctor who heals the patients suffering from the disease of bondage and suffering. The Guru is our spiritual doctor, who knows the best medicine for healing our spiritual maladies. Such a doctor is divine: "nidhayē sarva vidyānām." She never makes a mistake either in Her diagnosis or prescription of medicine.

ABODE OF THE DIVINE

Reminiscences

When I first met Amma in Amṛtapuri, I was studying the *śāstras* (scriptures) in an āśram in Bombay (now Mumbai). In Amṛtapuri, importance was given to tapas. I became attracted towards Amma's Dēvī Bhāva darśan and called it "Durgā Dēvī darśan." I became so emotional that I just wanted to remain here, but Amma said that I should first complete my studies and then return. At that time, many persons here had studied the śāstras and done arduous sādhana. I was one among those who, after studying for many years, used to feel incomplete inside.

Once, when Br. Śāntāmṛta Caitanya visited a Buddhist monastery in Japan, he found the environment, with its dense forests, mountains and gently flowing rivers, very pleasing. Everything there was beautiful, but the monk-in-charge said that the monastery lacked one thing: the presence of a *Bodhisattva*, a Self-realized soul. Śāntāmṛta said, "I will show you such a being."

And he did. Amma went there after about 10 years and presented the monk with a beautiful gift. Thereafter, he started progressing spiritually at a more rapid pace.

The late Ōṭṭūr Uṇṇi Nampūtirippāṭ, author of the *Aṣṭōttaram* (108 attributes) on Amma, was one of those people who had intuited Amma's divinity even from the initial days. He was very knowledgeable and learned. He used to call Amma "*Saccidānanda kaṭṭa*" — existence, knowledge and bliss in solid form.

When I came to stay in Amṛtapuri, there was just one room for meditation, a kitchen and the kaḷari. I used to stay in a small hut, which would leak during the monsoons.

In those days, the daily routine began with our waking up at 4:00 a.m. Arcana was at 5:00 a.m. Thereafter, instead of the morning tea, we would get a cup of diluted milk that contained a nominal amount of sugar. Then, there was śāstra class, followed by *haṭha yōga* and meditation. Amma would attend the meditation every day, sometimes supervising it.

At 9:30 a.m., breakfast was served. Each āśram resident would receive a modest serving of *kañji* (rice gruel); occasionally, we would receive one or two biscuits, chips or bananas, which devotees would bring.

Classes would resume at 11 a.m., when Amma would go for darśan, which would continue until about 2:00 p.m. Bhajans would start at 6:30 p.m. even then. In those days, there were not many musical instruments—only one set of *tablas* (Indian hand drums) and a harmonium. Nevertheless, bhajans were so full of devotion that Amma often used to soar into *samādhi*, a transcendental state in which one loses all sense of individual identity.

She used to give Dēvī Bhāva darśans on Sundays, Tuesdays and Thursdays. I was present during Her last Kṛṣṇa Bhāva darśan. In those days, Amma was slim, and She used to jump up very high many times.

Amma told us to keep a diary, which She would go through very carefully. One day, She wrote "*Nalla mōn*" ("Good son") in my diary and signed it.

When I reached Amṛtapuri for the first time, preparations for Amma's 33rd birthday were in full swing. The recording of the first '*Ōmkāra divya poruḷē*' was in progress. Amma's voice modulations—the ascent and descent—sounded to me like an airplane going up and coming down! In the 33rd stanza, Br. Bālu (now Swāmi Amṛtaswarupānanda) changed the tune a little, but Amma objected; She told him to retain the same tune. In those days, Amma gave utmost importance to *bhakti* (devotion); musical creativity was given lesser importance. It is not that She does not appreciate creativity; She wanted us to focus on God, and not let the music detract from this focus. Nevertheless, the bhajans then were beautiful, and many are evergreen compositions. The bhajans today are still rich in devotion, but to cater to the musical tastes of devotees, She sings songs that have mass appeal.

Water was scarce then and therefore invaluable. Amma would wake us all up early in the morning to collect water from the other side of the backwaters. She supervised all the work so that we would not inadvertently cause the neighbors any problem. Even after doing so much of work, we never felt tired. Life was hard, but we enjoyed each moment, even carrying heavy stones that would be used for construction, etc.

Often, we would accompany Amma for house visits, traveling in a 12-seater van. Amma would sit on the second seat and

Swāmi Rāmakṛṣṇānanda would drive the van. Some of us would sit on the laps of others for want of space.

I went back to Mumbai to complete my studies and returned after 10 months. Then I went to Kaṇṇūr. The following incident took place in 1986.

One of Amma's programs, which had been arranged at a Śiva temple in Kaṇṇūr, was cancelled at the last moment for various reasons. Another program was arranged at my pre-monastic home, which had a big verandah and a courtyard. Nearly 200 people took part.

There used to be two distinct groups in my pre-monastic home. One group, in which I was a member, would sing bhajans daily. The other group would spend a lot of time playing card games and drinking alcohol. To say that the outlook and interests of the two groups were at odds with each other would be an understatement. After Amma's visit, the activities of the second group ceased. Such is Amma's subtle yet powerfully benign influence.

Amma defines the word '*āśram*' as a composite of two words: '*ā*' and '*śramam*,' i.e. 'that effort.' What Amma means is the continuous effort until one attains the goal of human life—knowing one's own true nature as pure consciousness, which is beyond birth and death. Only by the Guru's grace can one gain this *jñāna* or Self-knowledge.

The compassionate Guru helps the disciple gain the necessary qualifications that will make him worthy to receive and assimilate Her teachings, which lead to liberation.

"Develop the innocence of a three-year-old child," Amma advises. Only one who is pure and innocent by nature can gain divine knowledge. Amma, the Guru, creates situations that make us childlike in Her presence. All of us are happy to say and feel, "I am Amma's child!" She encourages this attitude.

When it comes to becoming eligible for spiritual liberation, there are other qualities that are as important as childlike innocence. When Br. Srīkumār (now Swāmi Pūrṇamṛtānanda) first came to Amma, he said, "Amma, if there is a God, I want to kill Him! There is so much suffering in this world. Why does God give so much suffering to human beings?" Then a young engineering student, Br. Srīkumār was not well-versed with the scriptures yet. Amma removed all his doubts. This spiritual clarity is reflected in one of the bhajans he composed, *'Āzhikuḷḷil dinakaran maraññu:'* "The sun has set in the western ocean and the day has started its lament. It is but the play of the Universal Architect. This world, full of misery and sorrow, is but a drama of God."

Being aware of the suffering of others and trying to find solutions are noble qualities. A spiritual seeker must have them. A compassionate person alone is fit for liberation. Prince Siddhārtha became aware of worldly miseries and departed to the forest to find a permanent solution. He discovered God's presence within in the form of infinite peace and joy, and became the Buddha.

In one of the āśram bhajans, *'Ini oru janmam ivanēkolā Kṛṣṇa,'* the poet says, "O Kṛṣṇa, please do not give me another birth lest I fall into the deep quagmire of delusion." But later in the song, the poet declares, "If I should get another birth, may I be able to give Imperishable Joy to others and thus be of benefit to the world. If You permit me this, then give me any number of births as a human being!"

Amma sings many bhajans like this. In *'Vardē Vardē,'* a more recent bhajan, the poet says, "Give us eyes that see the sufferings of others, ears that listen to the sorrows of others, and a mind that is able to understand the sufferings of others!"

This prayer and attitude can help us become more expansive and see ourselves in others, thus making us grow in awareness. God is awareness; Amma is awareness—infinite awareness.

In the early days of the āśram, the brahmacārīs used to pray, *"Āpyāyantu mama angāni..."*—"May my limbs, sense organs and mind gain full strength so that they may see the Truth behind the Universe." Sanyāsīs who have gained Self-knowledge and are about to depart from the world pray boldly and joyfully, *"Vāyur amṛtam anilam atha idam bhasmāntam śarīram"*—"May my *prāṇas* (vital breaths) merge with the atmosphere and let my body be reduced to ashes" (because it has served its purpose). In the bhajan *'Rotē Jag Mē,'* which Amma sings, there is a particularly poignant line: "We come to earth crying, but we should leave it with a smile on our face."

This is possible only with the Guru's grace.

Always Amma's Child

When divine incarnations and other great sages are born, they sanctify their mothers' wombs. Thus, Lord Viṣṇu blessed Aditī, wife of Sage Kaśyapa, by being born in her womb as Vāmana. He blessed Kausalyā's womb by being born as Śrī Rāma, and Mother Dēvakī's womb by being born as Śrī Kṛṣṇa. Kausalyā and Dēvakī were celestial beings who had done a lot of tapas and prayed to God for the boon of begetting Him as their son. Other celestial beings also came down to earth just to give birth to great souls who sanctified the world. The Buddha's mother, Mahāmāyā, was one such person. She passed away within a short time of delivering the Buddha.

The scriptures say that God incarnates in every womb, and there are purification rites, rituals and vows called *samskāras* that purify both the would-be father and mother so that they can have virtuous offspring. In particular, the mother's womb is purified so as to make it a befitting receptacle for the divine. As mentioned earlier, Sage Kaśyapa and Aditī were the parents of Viṣṇu and also of other deities. Kaśyapa's second wife Ditī gave birth to *daityas*, the demons.

In 1962, two boys aged six and five respectively were staying in their hometown in North Kēraḷa with their grandparents; the children's parents were working in Chennai. In June 1963, when their mother, Remāmaṇī, returned home for her third delivery, she brought her young maidservant, Gaurī. Remāmaṇī gave birth to a baby girl on the early morning of July 16; her two older brothers excitedly named her Uṣā. That night, baby Uṣā passed away. Remāmaṇī passed away on August 8th, less than a month after the delivery. Gaurī, who was very attached to Remāmaṇī, was grief-stricken. She declared, "From now on, I will look after Remā-*akkā's*[26] sons and cook for them!"

Gaurī was very religious, like Remāmaṇī. Every day, she would get up early, bathe, say her prayers, and then cook for the children and grandparents. The two children grew up. I am the elder son. Notwithstanding the fact that my family was very religious, I used to wonder why I was so devoted to Śrī Karumārī-amman (the Tamil name for Goddess Pārvatī), even though I had stayed in Chennai, Tamil Nadu, for only a short time before joining Amma's āśram. It is quite possible that I assimilated this devotion through the food that Gaurī cooked for many years.

Many years ago, I accompanied Amma to a house in Chennai. When She sat down in the pūjā room, She noticed a picture of Karumārī-amman. Smiling and pointing to the photo, Amma said, "Satyātma's mother!" ('Satyātma' was my brahmacārī name.)

I replied, "But Karumārī-amman no longer holds the sword and trident!" I was alluding to the time when Amma used to wield them during Her Bhāva darśans.

I thank my earthly mother who gave me both this body and the good *samskāra* (inner values) that enabled me to come to the Divine Mother and be with Her for the rest of my life. All of Amma's children must thank their parents for giving them good samskāras, which brought them to Amma.

---

26 Akkā means older sister.

The most sacred womb is that of the Divine Mother. Shortly after I joined the āśram, I saw Amma holding babies on Her lap during ceremonies for naming them or giving them their first feed of solid food. I also wanted to sit on Amma's lap. I told Her that I wanted to be born as Her child. Amma laughed heartily and said, "Then I have to go and marry Śiva!"

I felt that I was troubling Her. So, I said, "It's okay if I am born to one of Your close devotees. Then You can put me on Your lap and feed me!" I said this with utmost sincerity and feeling, and Amma looked pleased. She used to tell other devotees about what I had said. She even spoke about it to devotees in the US when She went there for Her tour. Amma knew that the devotees would convey the news to me. And they did. Swāmi Pūrṇamṛtānanda sent a detailed e-mail about it as did two other devotees. I took it as a reminder from Amma to maintain the "I am always Her child" *bhāva* (devotional attitude). As Amma always says, "To know God, develop the innocence of a three-year-old child!"

In the last few years, before leaving for the Summer Tour of Japan and North America or the Fall Tour of Europe, Amma has come to the hall to make *dōśas* (Indian pancakes) for Her children. Eating the food that Amma has touched is purifying. Even during Her tours, both in India and abroad, Amma delights in feeding Her children. Every child likes to eat food cooked by its mother; nothing satisfies him or her more.

Only a mother can really satisfy her child's hunger. When she cooks for her children, she does so with love. The food is saturated not only with her love but her qualities also. Children who eat food cooked by their mothers develop their mother's qualities and a strong bond of love with their mothers. When we eat food cooked in a restaurant, the samskāra of the cooks there seeps into us through the food. Restaurants are interested in making profits, and eating food cooked in such an environment causes the money-making, commercial vibration to affect our mind.

Once, a rich devotee invited a well-known sanyāsī for a feast. The sanyāsī agreed to come, but on the day of the feast, he had to attend to an important task in his āśram. He sent one of his senior disciples to the devotee's house. The disciple was treated to a sumptuous feast. While eating, the disciple discovered, to his horror, that he was beset by an irresistible urge to steal a silver cup on the table. Unable to control this strange, negative desire, he stole it!

That night, his guilty conscience did not let him sleep. He got up, went to his Guru, and confessed, "O Guru, I committed an unpardonable crime. I stole an expensive cup from the devotee. Please forgive me and advise me on what to do."

The sanyāsī calmly replied, "Go to the host's house tomorrow, return the cup, and ask for his forgiveness."

The disciple did as his Guru had advised. The host was shocked. He asked the sanyāsī, "Swāmiji, how can your disciple do such a thing?" The sanyāsī asked him who had cooked the food given to the disciple. Embarrassed, the host said, "Swāmiji, my wife was having her monthly period, and so, a woman who lives near our house cooked the food."[27] The sanyāsī asked the devotee to inquire into the cook's background. To his surprise, he learned that she had the habit of stealing! The food she cooked had absorbed this negative quality, thus affecting the disciple.

27 In orthodox Indian homes, women do not cook during their menstrual periods.

Always Amma's Child But Growing in Wisdom

When I was in school, I read Shakespeare's famous poem, 'Seven Stages of Man.'

All the world's a stage,
And all the men and women merely players...
... At first the infant,
Mewling and puking in the nurse's arms;
And then the whining schoolboy, with his satchel
And shining morning face, creeping like snail
Unwillingly to school...

Shakespeare describes man's last stage as "second childishness and mere oblivion, sans teeth, sans eyes, sans taste, sans everything." The Bard's description is very true with respect to the world in general. A baby's awareness is minimal; it has relatively little body consciousness, and is only aware of its own hunger and thirst, and cries when it feels hungry or thirsty. As the child grows, its awareness expands. It becomes increasingly conscious. Through the sense organs and the mind, the child perceives more of the world around it.

But physical growth is not indefinite. Well before middle age, the body starts to weaken and the sense organs begin to deteriorate. In the infirmity of old age, one lies in bed helplessly like a baby, needing assistance and support for everything, even attending the calls of nature. Shakespeare's understanding of human life—its limitation and impermanence—was clear, even philosophic.

In *The Tempest*, he wrote:

> The cloud-capp'd towers, the gorgeous palaces,
> The solemn temples, the great globe itself,
> Yea, all which it inherit, shall dissolve,
> And, like this insubstantial pageant faded,
> Leave not a rack behind...

In his time, there were no 'cloud-capp'd buildings.' How did he know that there would be skyscrapers in the future? Shakespeare's observations and conclusions were poignant and deep, and his prescience marvelous! In the verse above, he points to the transience of the created world. Not only living beings, but the earth itself will perish one day. The *Purāṇas* speak similarly of *praḷaya*, when all of creation will dissolve into Lord Viṣṇu.

Indian culture posits 'four stages of man,' *viz. brahmacārya* (celibate student-hood), *gārhasthya* (householder life), *vānaprastha* (retired life) and *sanyāsa* (renunciation). The Indian conception of the final stage of life is that of freedom—total liberation from all worldly bondages and desires. In this state, one has complete awareness, which is the polar opposite of Shakespeare's 'mere oblivion.' The one who takes us to spiritual liberation is the Guru, who molds disciples and devotees so that they attain maximum growth.

Years ago, a devotee passed the following comment on the senior sanyāsīs of the āśram: "The swāmis still think they are children and are playful. They have not grown up!"

Responding to this, Swāmi Amṛtaswarupānanda said, "I am very sorry to say that we refuse to grow up! We are children, Amma's little children for life!"

Those who constantly think of Amma and Her infinite nature can never feel that they are big or grownup; they are always like children.

A non-believer once asked, "Why is Mother Kāḷī not properly dressed?"

I replied, "When a mother comes out of the bathroom after her bath and sees her three-month-old baby on the bed, she does not bother to dress quickly, but when a grownup son knocks on the door, the mother says, "Coming, son!" and hurriedly puts on her clothes.

In the Divine Mother's presence, who is a grownup? We are all just babies. As Amma's children, let us learn to become small. She is the ocean, and we are pieces of ice floating on that ocean. Let us melt, becoming smaller and smaller, and eventually dissolve completely into Her.

Temples in India, especially those in the South, are magnificent, and the decorations of the main idols are truly resplendent. Seeing them, even a king would feel that he was in the presence of God. "He is everything. I am nothing!"—this should be the firm conviction of every devotee.

A devotee once asked me, "Is it necessary to go to temples? My father taught me to pray at home with sincerity and devotion."

First, let me congratulate the father who taught his son to pray thus. Nowadays, many fathers do not do that! I lost my earthly mother when I was just six years old, but before she passed away, she had already taught my brother and me to sing bhajans everyday after sunset.

The answer to the question is: if, while sitting at home, you have been able to expand your mind to realize the entire universe as God's family, visiting the temple is not necessary. However, if you are not able to expand your mind in spite of regularly going to temples, your temple visits have not served their purpose.

At home, we pray for the well-being of our family—"O Amma! Bless *my* father, *my* mother, *my* brothers and *my* sisters." Satgurus like Amma teach us to expand our 'my'ness to include the entire universe. They make us understand that all beings in this universe are interconnected and interdependent, and that 'my happiness' is dependent on the happiness of all other beings. Amma teaches us this universal truth. That is why we chant the mantra '*lōkāḥ samastāh sukhinō bhavantu*' ('May all beings in all the worlds be happy').

Let us chant this mantra with sincerity and devotion, and, finally, like camphor melting and becoming one with the atmosphere, may we, too, melt in the fire of wisdom and devotion and become one with the all-pervading Supreme Being.

Shakespeare's second childishness is a state of helplessness and dependence—dying and being born again to continue the misery of worldly existence. In contrast, the second childishness of the spiritually awakened is full of ever-expanding awareness, childlike purity, simplicity and innocence, and wealth of wisdom. O Amma, bless Your children so that we may merge into eternity, infinite peace and infinite joy. May we always be Your children, but ever growing in wisdom.

Like Beads on a String

At the dawn of 2004, Amma posed a question to all those gathered for the New Year celebrations in Amṛtapuri: "How can we contribute to minimizing global conflicts and agitation?"

She called out a few names, asking them to come forward and answer. My name was one of them. One by one, the devotees started responding.

One of them said, "The only way we can contribute to reducing global agitation is by checking, controlling and correcting ourselves!"

Some of the students of our Computer and Engineering institutes prayed to Amma to give them the strength not to repeat the mistakes they had knowingly and unknowingly committed in the previous year.

Another devotee said, "We have to be like a football team; in order to win, there must be collective effort and team spirit."

I was listening and at the same time mentally preparing what I intended to say.

I first remembered Amma's teaching. Years back, She said that a spiritual seeker is like a good businessperson who checks the profit-and-loss account at the end of each day, week, month and year. As spiritual seekers, we should check how much worship, meditation and service we have done. We should also consider how much purification has taken place within us, which can be measured by the amount of peace and joy we experience in our day-to-day life and by how relaxed we are in trying circumstances.

There is a beautiful incident in Tulsīdās's *Rāmcaritmanas.* When Lakṣmaṇa killed Indrajit, Rāvaṇa's son, Indrajit uttered, "O Rāma! O Lakṣmaṇa!" Hearing this, Hanumān and Angad (Vali's son) felt their hair standing on end. They cried out, "O Indrajit, blessed indeed is your mother, who gave birth to a son like you who remembered Rāma at the time of death!"

If we want to become worthy of being called Amma's children, let us constantly remember the Divine Mother. Only then can we remember Her when we leave our earthly bodies.

My mind went back to the first answer—checking, controlling and correcting ourselves—and to the second—putting forth the collective effort and having the team spirit of a football team. How true, I thought! As Amma's children, each one of us must try to set the best example as individuals who are part of a family, society, a country and the world. One weak link in a chain makes the entire chain weak. One musician playing a wrong note affects the harmony of the entire orchestra. One soldier dressed in civilian clothes during a parade spoils the uniformed beauty of the entire contingent.

Amma Herself gives a beautiful example: we, Her children, must be like the keys of a harmonium. Its 40-odd keys are extremely close, as if they form a single frame. Though they seem to touch each other, they actually don't! For this reason, when one key is pressed, the ones next to it do not respond and create a disturbance in the music. So, too, Amma's children have to be very close because we are members of one family. But at the same time, we should not be attached to each other, because we are all spiritual seekers. "Love everyone without attachment" – this is what Amma teaches.

Amma, the divine musician, creates divine music from the harmonium made up of keys known as devotees. Let us pray to Her that the divine vibrations of the music She creates pervades the entire universe! May all humanity hear it, clap their hands and, dancing to Her tune, move forward to eternal peace and happiness.

Saving Grace

There are occasions when Amma reveals Her omniscience, even though She has not studied the Vēdic scriptures, *Purāṇas* or other scriptural texts. When I first joined the āśram, Amma used to say, "Children, do not ask for anything less than *Ātma-sākṣātkāram* (Self-realization)." It indicated that She knows the essence of the Vēdic teaching—knowledge of the *Ātma*, the Self—and that She is capable of taking us to that supreme state.

I had a direct experience of Amma's all-knowing nature when She told me once, "Son, I haven't learnt the Vēdas. So, whatever I say may be like the croaking of a frog. You have studied the scriptures. So, talk to the āśram residents."

I was amazed because Amma had just alluded to the *Māṇḍūkya Upaniṣad*, the most difficult among the Upaniṣads, which teaches us to realize the eternal Ātma and to renounce all worldly objects and relationships because they are false. For most people, this advice is difficult and even unpleasant to hear, like the croaking of a frog. '*Māṇḍūkya*' means frog.

The '*Mā – Ōm*' meditation that Amma teaches—in which one mentally intones "Mā" while inhaling and "Ōm" while exhaling—is also indicative of Her all-knowing nature. The *Kaṭhōpaniṣad* says, "He who chants 'Ōm' while leaving the body reaches *Brahmalōka*" (2.17). If we make a habit of chanting "Mā - Ōm," we will naturally chant "Ōm" when the last breath leaves our body, and thus we will go to the highest world.

A fisherman was sitting on a rock on the banks of a river. He was holding his fishing rod and patiently waiting for a fish to nibble the bait. Suddenly, he heard a scream—someone had fallen into the river. The fisherman ran towards the sound, and saw a man frantically waving his hands in the waters. The fisherman tied a small bag to the fishing hook, threw the bag towards the drowning man and shouted, "Grab it!" The drowning man grabbed it and was pulled to the safety of the shore.

The thin, nylon thread connecting the fishing rod to the hook is almost invisible and yet so strong that no fish can pull and break it! The drowning man was saved by such a thread! He knew its strength and had the good sense to grab it.

Amma's darśan is like this. When there is big crowd, each devotee might get about 15 seconds of Her divine touch and words of comfort. But that is enough! After one has received darśan, one should go and sit in the hall or any quiet place, close the eyes and let the experience sink in deeply instead of dissipating the divine energy by engaging in idle talk or activity.

An old devotee, who is a good teacher of communication skills and is working in one of Amma's MBA colleges, says, "In 15 seconds, Amma creates a strong bond with the devotees who come for Her darśan! There is no modern course on communication skills in the whole world that can train you to win over people's friendship and faith in 15 seconds!"

This is not to say that 15 seconds with Amma are enough. We must allow the impact of the darśan to sink deep within so that the memory becomes clearer and stronger, and so that thoughts of Amma become longer, stronger and continuous. One should also never miss an opportunity to sit near Amma when possible. The Guru's physical presence has no equal; there is no other *sādhana* (spiritual practice) that can purify so deeply.

Every year, on the eve of Amma's Birthday, one of the senior swāmis goes to the aśram kitchen to light a lamp in front of Amma's photo. Huge pots and cauldrons would have already been placed on fire pits ready to cook for the hundreds of thousands of devotees attending Amma's birthday celebrations. From this lamp, an oil-soaked wick is lit and used to light all the fire pits. That one spark of fire thus becomes the fire that cooks for so many people.

The 15-second darśan is like a small flame that can grow into a blazing fire of intense devotion, which can burn away the accumulated burden of prārabdha accumulated over many past lives! This fire of devotion also kindles divine inspiration, enthusiasm and strength to serve the world and bring more people to Amma.

In the *Bhagavad Gītā*, Lord Kṛṣṇa says,

svalpamapyasya dharmasya
trāyatē mahatō bhayāt

Even a little of this divine knowledge protects one from great fear. (2.40)

A drunkard was once crossing the road on his way to his usual drinking booth. He saw Śrī Caitanya Mahāprabhu[28] and his devotees singing and dancing their way towards him. Because he liked dancing, he thought, "Let me join the dance. Afterwards, I will go and drink!" He joined the group and danced with them until they reached a temple. By the time he left, the watering hole he frequented had closed, and so, he returned home. The next day, the same thing happened—he joined the dancing, reached the temple, and then returned home. This happened day after day. Within a short time, the man started looking forward to dancing with the group singing devotional songs. Not seeing him anymore at the watering hole, his old friends asked him why he was not coming there. Smiling, he told them, "I have found a new intoxication, that of *bhakti* (devotion). The old intoxication is nothing compared to this one!"

Drinking starts with a mug, and might develop into a habit, which finally drowns the drinker. Bhakti also starts with a little sip. The measure increases. If one keeps imbibing the divine name, one merges into the ocean of bliss. The waves of bliss gradually carry one to the other shore of Immortality!

When devotees go on pilgrimages to sacred places, the wise ones among them sit or walk quietly and let the experience of the place sink deeply into them. They then return, purified with the memory of the sacred places imprinted deep in their hearts. The others capture what they see on their phones. And thus,

---

28 A saint (1486 – 1534 CE) who advocated the path of devotion to Lord Kṛṣṇa as the means to attain perfection in life.

Vṛndāvan and Bōdh Gayā[29] remain only on their phones or in their laptops!

Many devotees of Amma save photos or videos of Amma, and messages from Her that they receive through WhatsApp. It is certainly good to save these images and teachings in our phones. Let us also imprint them in our hearts. For then, we will be truly saved. *'Svalpam api'*—even a little of Amma is enough to save us from drowning in the ocean of worldliness.

I remember a short video that I had saved in my heart. An elderly ācārya asks his little brahmacārī disciples,

> *āpadi kim karaṇīyam?*
>
> What must one do when one is in danger?

The little ones reply,

> *smaraṇīyam caraṇayugaḷam ambāyāh!*
>
> One should remember the holy feet of Ambā, the Divine Mother!

And the compassionate Divine Mother comes rushing to the rescue of Her Beloved children!

Let us never think that Amma is far away. Amma says as much:

> *illa ōmane, illa jñān ninnil nin*
> *orunāḷum akannu pōkayilla!*

---

29 Bōdh Gayā is the place where Lord Buddha attained spiritual enlightenment.

> Never, my beloved child, never will I forsake you and go far away!

Amma is *'hṛdayanivāsini'*—She dwells in our hearts. If this understanding of *'svalpamapyasya dharmasya'*—that Amma is always with us—takes firm root in our minds, then *'trāyatē mahatō bhayāt'*—we will be protected from great fear.

Where Amma Is, There Amṛtapuri Is.

It was dawn, but the rising sun seemed to hesitate. The people of Ayōdhyā were praying that the sun would never rise because daybreak would take away from them the life and soul of Ayōdhyā—Śrī Rāma. It was the day that Lord Rāma, His wife, Sītā, and His brother, Lakṣmaṇa, would leave the kingdom for the forest. The whole of Ayōdhyā was plunged in gloom. Many were agitated at the injustice meted out to Rāma, their God in human form.

Only three faces shone with divine peace—those of Rāma, Sītā and Lakṣmaṇa. Members of the Sūrya dynasty, they cared little for luxury, sensual enjoyments or personal comforts. They all had only one thought in mind: *dharma* (righteousness). Lord Rāma was the very personification of dharma. As for the others in His family, even Vālmīki, the illustrious author of the *Rāmāyaṇa*, would have been at a loss to say who excelled the others in nobility and character.

The *Rāmāyaṇa* contains many subtle teachings and truths that can guide the human race to the ultimate goal of God-realization. Sumitrā, Lakṣmaṇa's mother, was the wisest among the queens, though the youngest. She encouraged her son to follow Rāma to the forest and to serve Him. She said, "Where Śrī Rāma is, there alone Ayōdhyā is. O son, go with my blessings. May you be peaceful!"

If Ayōdhyā is where Lord Rāma is, is Amṛtapuri where Amma is? Amma's children will answer this question in different ways, but all will agree on one point. In Amma's physical absence, Amṛtapuri is just not the same. Her physical presence is like bright sunshine—illumining and nourishing. In Her physical absence, Amṛtapuri seems gloomy in comparison. We can see how even nature in Amṛtapuri seems to become still and downcast a few days before Amma's departure, and how it brightens up a few days before Her arrival. Where Amma is, there nature itself joins Her children in making the place festive.

Nevertheless, there is something special about Amṛtapuri. All of Amma's children who accompany Her on Her Indian Tour, as well as those who follow Her abroad, are happy to return to Amṛtapuri—home, sweet home!

From Ayōdhyā, Lord Rāma started walking towards the South, all the way to Lanka. The places where the Lord rested, stayed and worshipped became sacred spots. It is our duty to preserve them to the best of our ability. The Śrī Lankans have preserved many places connected with the *Rāmāyaṇa*: Aśōka Vana, where Sītā was held captive and where Hanumān met Her, and the place where the *vānara sēna* (army of monkeys) landed, among others. Notwithstanding all these pilgrim destinations, Ayōdhyā remains the most important pilgrimage destination for Rāma devotees. No other sacred place can be compared to Ayōdhyā.

Similarly, Lord Kṛṣṇa was born and grew up in Gōkul. He later moved to Mathura, where He undertook an '*Amala Bhāratam*' (Clean India) campaign of sorts, exterminating the garbage of Kamsa and his demonic tribe. How many such Amala Bhāratam Campaigns the Avatārs of the past have done!

The very purpose of Amma's birth is Amala Bhāratam—cleaning human communities not only in India but all around the world of garbage in the form of selfishness, greed and ego. Reading the *Dēvī Māhātmyam*, one can see how many Amala Bhāratams Dēvī, the Goddess, launched! She cleared the land of garbage in the form of demons like Madhu-Kaitabha, Śumbha-Niśumbha and, finally, Mahiṣāsura and their tribes. After every Amala Bhāratam campaign, not only human beings but the gods also were able to breathe fresh air. With hearts full of gratitude, devotion and infinite joy, they praised Dēvī,

> *sarva mangala māngalyē śivē sarvārtha sādhikē*
> *śaranyē tryambakē gauri nārayaṇi namōstutē*
>
> We bow down to You, O Nārayaṇi (consort of Lord Viṣṇu), who is the essence of all that is auspicious, who bestows prosperity, who is the sole refuge, one with three eyes and a beautiful face!

Lord Kṛṣṇa stayed in Mathura for some time with His parents and grandparents. But there is a difference between Mathura and Gōkul. No other place cried like Gōkul in Kṛṣṇa's physical absence! In Rāma's physical absence, no place shed as many tears as Ayōdhyā! In Amma's physical absence, no other place cries like Amṛtapuri! Many of Amma's branch āśrams are heavens on earth—peaceful and charged with the divine presence. Nevertheless, Amṛtapuri is unique, the nucleus of spiritual vibrations.

During a recent Brahmasthānam festival at Triśśūr, a devotee narrated her soul-stirring experience with Amma. Many years before, this devotee had come for darśan when Amma used to give Bhāva Darśan in the kaḷari. While gazing at Amma, she saw Amma's face turning into that of Kāḷī or Cāmuṇḍī (a form of the Divine Mother), who has two long teeth descending from the upper gum. However, Amma's two long teeth ascended upward from Her lower jaw. The devotee was overcome with devotion at this vision, but at the same time puzzled over the unusual features of Amma's face.

A few days later, she went to the Paramara Dēvī Temple in Kochi. There, she saw a picture of Dēvī who looked exactly like Amma during Her Dēvī Bhāva darśan! In all of Dēvī's *raudra* (ferocious) forms, Her canines descend from Her upper jaw, except for Vārāhī, the feminine power of Varāha, Viṣṇu's boar incarnation. The *Nārayaṇi Stutī* in the 11th chapter of *Dēvī Māhātmyam* declaims,

> *gṛhitōgra mahācakrē*
> *danṣṭrōddhṛta vasundharē*
> *varāha rūpiṇī śivē,*
> *nārayaṇi namōstutē!*
>
> Prostrations to you, O Nārayaṇi, O Śivē, who raised the earth with Your tusks of perseverance, wielding the great discus of revolving time, O auspicious Dēvī, with a boar-like form! (17)

During Amma's 60th birthday, there were pictures of Viṣṇu's Varāha Avatār at all the four entrances of hall where the

Mahācaṇḍikā Hōma[30] was being performed. As mentioned earlier, Lord Viṣṇu had assumed the lowly form of a boar to raise the earth from the ocean. He is called '*Yajña Varāha.*' Any act undertaken for the uplift of the world is called a *yajña.*[31] Like the divine boar, we must be ready to do any work for the uplift of the world. Wasn't Amma showing the devotee that She has come to uplift the world and reinstate dharma? Many other devotees visiting Amṛtapuri have had similar experiences of Amma's divine nature.

Swāmi Amṛtaswarupānanda narrated to me the experience of a seven-year-old boy at one of Amma's centers in the USA. Amma's Dēvī Bhāva darśan was about to end. She stood up as usual and slowly walked to the front of the stage. Usually, Amma showers flowers on Her devotees, standing with a divine smile for some time, and then slowly, Her eyes take on a distant look, cast slightly upwards. At that time, the boy, who was holding his father's hand, suddenly said, "Dad, I can see many grand-looking people, tall, with long hair and beards! I can also see many handsome men and beautiful women dressed gorgeously like kings and queens. They are all looking on Amma with palms joined together prayerfully."

The little boy had seen *ṛṣis* (sages) and *dēvas* (deities) and their feminine powers, all of whom had come for Amma's darśan. Amma Herself has said that such beings come for Her darśan. Whether in Amṛtapuri or in the USA, She is the same. We

30 Ritual wherein an oblation or religious offering is made into a sacrificial fire.

31 Vēdic ritual performed before a sacred fire.

perceive Amma according to the power of our instruments, *viz.* our eyes, ears and mind. If the sun came just a little closer to the earth, we would be scorched to death! Similarly, our body-mind equipment has only a limited capacity. Amma manifests only as much power as we can perceive with our limited senses and mind. Those who have performed a lot of austerities know Amma better. Most of Amma's children find Amṛtapuri, which is charged with spiritual vibrations, the best place for austerities. It is incomparable! Amma Herself has said that Amṛtapuri is the place where great sages once performed tapas. Thus, it is *tapō bhūmi* (abode of austerities), *karma bhūmi* (abode of selfless action) and *mōkṣa bhūmi* (abode of spiritual liberation).

DIVINE RIDDLES

Ammē Bhagavatī Nitya Kanyē Dēvī

Many years ago, during a recording of a bhajan, Amma said something thought-provoking. She quoted the first line of an old bhajan:

> *ammē bhagavatī nitya kanyē dēvī*
>
> O Mother, Supreme Ruler, O Goddess, who is ever a virgin.

Dēvī is a Mother, yet a virgin. Every being in this universe has come about only through a union of a male and a female. But Mother Pārvatī created Her first and foremost son, Gaṇēśa, with the sandalwood paste on Her own body. Lord Śiva created Muruga through His divine, third eye.

The word for 'creation' in Sanskrit is '*sṛṣṭi*.' The root of the word is '*sṛj*,' which means 'to project.' Like visuals projected on a screen, all of creation is only a projection; it is only a manifestation of the Universal Mother's *māyāśaktī* (power of illusion).

Amma also says, "Children, the Creator and creation are not two, but one." The Divine Mother does not need materials and instruments for creating this universe. It manifested from Her own cosmic body.

The *Muṇḍaka Upaniṣad* illustrates this point with a beautiful example.

> *yathorṇanābhi sṛjatē gṛhnatē ca...*
>
> As the spider emits and retracts the web... (1.1.7)

In the same bhajan, *'Ammē bhagavatī nitya kanyē,'* there is the following line:

> *tān onnum ceyyade sarvam ceytīḍunna*
>
> Without doing anything, Dēvī alone does everything.

But another bhajan that Amma sings declares,

> *nī ceyyum karmangaḷ ōrōnnum mānuṣar*
> *tān ceyvatennu tān ōrkkayallō*
>
> Every action is done by you, O Dēvī, but human beings think they are doing it.

This appears to be a contradiction. One bhajan says Dēvī does not do anything, but another bhajan says She alone does everything. If we think about this deeply, we can see that there is no contradiction.

Take the case of electricity. Electrical equipment functions because of it. The electricity does not do anything, but in its 'presence,' the bulb gives light, the fan, air, and the stove, heat. This is similar to what is implied when we say that without doing anything, Dēvī alone does everything.

But if the bulb thinks, "I am illuminating the place by my power!" or if the fan thinks, "I am giving air to everyone!" it is ignorance. Similarly, if we think that we perform actions with our power, we are mistaken; hence, the lyrics of the other bhajan.

The following mantras appear in the *Viṣṇu Sahasranāma* (1,000 names of Lord Viṣṇu):

lōkādhyakṣaḥ surādhyakṣaḥ dharmādhyakṣaḥ kṛtākrithaḥ

Viṣṇu is the presiding power of all the worlds, all gods, all action, and of cause and effect. (133 - 136)

I bear this line in mind when called upon to preside over functions or asked to deliver the presidential address. I say, "We have lit the lamp. The *dīpam* (flame) represents Amma, Ādiparāśaktī (the Primal, Supreme Power), and She alone is the *adhyakṣa* (presiding power)."

Our beloved Amma has inspired thousands of Her beloved children to do selfless service. Let us remember that whatever we have done is only because of Her infinite grace, power and compassion.

Ōm vidyā-avidyā svarūpiṇyai namaḥ

During a recent meditation session, Amma asked, "Children, what is the meaning of '*vidyā-avidyā svarūpiṇī?*'[32] How can Dēvī be of the form of both knowledge and ignorance?"

This was yet another one of Amma's *līlās* (divine sport) to guide us deep into the nature of Dēvī, the Goddess, i.e. Amma's real nature. Most of us know Amma's *rūpam*, Her outer form, which we see in front of us. But to know Amma's *svarūpam*, Her essential, cosmic, imperishable nature, the only way is to surrender to Her totally. She will then reveal to us Her real nature.

Knowledge and ignorance are opposed to each other, like light and darkness. Where there is light, there cannot be darkness; where there is knowledge, ignorance cannot exist. How then can Amma or Dēvī be both knowledge (*vidyā*) and ignorance (*avidyā*)? How can both be Her svarūpam?

When Amma asked us this question, we did not know the answer; i.e. we experienced ignorance, avidyā, in our minds. And when we get the right answer, our ignorance is replaced by knowledge, understanding, revelation and conviction—in other words, vidyā. In both instances, there is awareness—either of ignorance or of understanding.

The three levels of experience we are familiar with are the waking state (in which we experience the outer world of forms), the dream state (in which we experience an inner world created

---

32 Ōm vidyā-avidyā swarūpiṇyai namaḥ = Salutations to the Divine Mother, who is of the form of both knowledge and ignorance. (Laḷitā Sahasranāma, 402)

by our own mind), and the deep sleep or dreamless sleep state (wherein one experiences blissful nothingness, an absence of everything). We express our experience of this last state by saying, "I didn't know anything!" or "I was aware of nothing!" The technical name for this state of ignorance is *tamas*. Dēvī is *triguṇātmika*, i.e. one who wields three types of power or forms, viz. *satva*, *rajas* and tamas. Tamas is associated with lethargy, indolence or inactivity; rajas, with passion and activity; and satva, with light and understanding. We helplessly shunt back and forth from satva to rajas and tamas, and back again to rajas and satva. We have only three levels of experiences—waking, dream and deep sleep. But there is another state:

> *vēdāhamētam puruṣam mahāntam*
> *āditya varṇam tamasaḥ parastāt*
>
> I have known that Supreme Being, glorious like the sun and beyond all darkness. (*Puruṣa Sūktam*, 2)

There is a beautiful hymn in praise of Dēvī known as '*Dēvī Atharva Śīrṣam*,' which appears in the *Atharva Vēda*. A part of the *Dēvī Atharva Śīrṣam*, the '*Ṛg Vēdiya Dēvī Sūktam*,' teaches that everything in this universe is Dēvī's form and energy, that every manifestation is Dēvī's—both that which manifests as knowledge and ignorance. The *Dēvī Atharva Śīrṣam* hails Dēvī as the one, all-pervading reality appearing as the entire creation with its countless forms of living and non-living beings. When Dēvī appears before the dēvas in Her Divine form, they are unable to understand Her. They ask, "*Kā asi tvam?*" – "Who are you, O effulgent being?"

Dēvī explains Her true reality to the dēvas.

aham brahmasvarūpiṇī
mattaḥ prakṛti
puruṣātmakam jagat

I am the all-pervading Brahman. From Me alone has arisen this creation filled with sentient and non-sentient beings. (2)

In the fourth verse, She says,

vidyā aham avidyā aham

I am knowledge as well as ignorance.

Thus, any form of experience that takes place within our minds and bodies is Her form.

Just as Śrī Kṛṣṇa teaches Arjuna, elaborating His glories in various places from chapters 7 to 11, Śrī Dēvī also tells the dēvas that, beginning from Brahma, Viṣṇu and Śiva, the Hindu Trinity, and including both positive and negative powers in the world, "I alone appear as all these powers. They all come from Me and merge into Me."

With bowed heads and folded hands, the Dēvas then praise Dēvī.

durgām dēvīm śaraṇam prapadyāmahē,
asurān nāśayitryai tē namaḥ

> We take refuge in Durgā Dēvī, who is the destroyer of *asuras* (demons). (9)

But in the 17th verse, the gods declare,

> *sā eśāyātu dhāna*
> *asura rakṣāmsi piśāca*
> *yakṣāh siddhāh*
>
> She (Dēvī) alone has become every being, including the negative (evil) forces like *asuras*, *rākṣas*, *piśācis*, *yakṣas* and the powerful *siddhas.*[33]

To say that Dēvī alone became the asuras and that She alone destroys them might sound contradictory. If this seeming contradiction or confusion is cleared, then we can understand the narrations in the *Dēvī Māhātmyam*, and we will not feel disturbed when we read about the number of asuras Goddess Durgā destroyed.

Dēvī Māhātmyam is an epic poem of destruction. If people say, "The Universe Mother is compassionate, but there is only destruction in Her Avatārs and līlās!" how would we respond?

Remember the mantra "*Ōm mahāgrāsāyai namaḥ!*" from the *Laḷitā Sahasranāma*? It means, "I bow to the Divine Mother, who is the great devourer" (752). Mahakāḷī swallows everything at the end of the *kalpa* (cycle of creation). Consider the example Amma gives of gold and gold ornaments. Mahakāḷī is like gold, the permanent reality, and the countless forms in the creation are

33 Fiends who are antagonistic to God and the good.

like gold ornaments. The Universal Mother destroying the asuras is like the gold ornaments merging into gold. Does destruction really take place? No. When gold 'swallows' gold ornaments, gold alone remains. Similar is the Divine Mother's annihilation. The countless forms merge into their source, Ādiparāśaktī, the Primal Supreme Power. Asuras manifested from Her tamasic aspect.

'Devil' minus 'L' = 'Dēvī.' This equation is hard to believe, but true! We learn in chemistry that both charcoal and diamonds are carbon. Similarly, every one of us is made of the same substance. If we purge the devil of lethargy, lawlessness, lust, lies, loose talk and licentiousness, it will become pure and merge into Dēvī.

Some religions hold God as eternally good and the devil as permanently bad. In John Milton's 'Paradise Lost,' a sinner "falls like Lucifer never to hope again." In Hinduism, there is hope for everyone. Even devilish beings are purified, after which, they merge into the Supreme Being.

In some religions, the Lord of Hell is wicked and opposed to God and the good, but in Hinduism, the Lord of Hell is Yamadēv, son of Sūrya (Sun) and brother of Śani (Saturn) and Yamunā, the sacred river. He is an ardent devotee of Lord Viṣṇu and a servant of Lord Śiva. The most vicious devils like Hiraṇyakāśipu, Hiraṇyākṣa and Rāvaṇa were incarnations of the brothers Jaya and Vijaya—doorkeepers at Vaikuṇṭha, the celestial abode of Lord Viṣṇu—whom sages had cursed to be born as asuras. When one's *tamas* increases, one gets an asuric body. But inevitably, everyone is purified. All the demons killed by the Avatārs of Viṣṇu and Dēvī merged into them. We call asuras and rākṣasas wicked and hate them. Amma calls them impure, showers them with compassion, and leads them to purity.

Some of us have the habit of permanently blacklisting people. This is wrong. Even the worst sinners are purified and can attain liberation in Amma's divine presence. Brahma manifested from the eternal Viṣṇu. From Brahma manifested Sage Kaśyapa. The gods manifested from Aditī, one of Kaśyapa's wives. From his other wife, Ditī, the asuras came into being. In other words, both gods and demons have same source—Ādiparāśaktī, primordial energy, and Viṣṇu, all-pervading consciousness.

Dēvī alone appears in every form and She alone is the source into which every form merges. At the end of the *Dēvī Atharva Śīrṣam*, Dēvī is called '*śūnya sākṣiṇī*'—one who is witness to a state of nothingness, when the entire creation merges into Her. But even when everything disappears, Dēvī remains, a witness to the appearance and disappearance of every being.

Similarly, both vidyā and avidyā exist in awareness. Awareness is Amma's real nature. She wants us to know Her completely. When we do so, we will understand that we are always one with Her and not different from Her.

How do we start to know Her? Let us cultivate a liking for silence. When we chant the *Laḷitā Sahasranāma*, for example, the sounds of chanting merge into silence; we become aware that sound merges into silence. Both sound and silence exist in pure awareness.

Let us meditate deeply. Only a living spiritual master can take us deep into our real nature. With Her grace, let us become one with Amma.

Dualities... and going beyond them.

For youth and even many elders in India, their source of Purāṇic knowledge is the cinema. Many have formed an impression of who or what Ādiparāśaktī is from what they have seen on the big screen. A movie on Ādiparāśaktī begins with lightning, thunder, rain, violent storm, planets and galaxies appearing and disappearing, and explosive fireworks! Movie makers, with their limited understanding of the Purāṇas, highlight only one aspect of Parāśaktī. They do not know the most important aspect, Her *jñāna śaktī*, the power of Her all-knowing nature.

The *Durgā Sūktam* starts with "*Ōm jātavēdasē...*" which means "O Dēvī, who illumines and knows everything." The *Śrī Sūktam* says, "*Candram hiraṇmayīm lakṣmīm jātavēdo ma āvaḥ.*" Here, too, Lakṣmī is called 'jātavēda.'

Some devotees are confused when they hear that both good and bad come from the same source: the Supreme Being. The Guru's grace and a deep understanding are required to realize this Truth. In all other religions, good and bad are held to be opposite, but in Sanātana Dharma,[34] good and bad are relative.

In the beginning of our spiritual life, we give up the bad and accept only the good, but at the end of our spiritual journey, we go beyond good, too.

Good and bad are relative. Is it good to chant the *Laḷitā Sahasranāma?* Devotees would agree that it is good, without doubt.

---

34 Literally, 'Eternal Religion' or 'The Eternal Way of Life,' the original and traditional name for Hinduism.

Recently, when Amma called all āśram residents for a meeting in the Kāḷī Temple, and was dispensing advice and instructions, one person was chanting the *Laḷitā Sahasranāma.* This is bad! When the Guru is talking to us, we must be totally focused on Her; nothing else is more important. Therefore, what is good at a particular place and time may be bad at another place and time.

Shakespeare wrote, "There is nothing either good or bad, but thinking makes it so" (*Hamlet*, 2.2). When I first read it as a student, I was surprised and did not understand it at all! But now, I am slowly beginning to understand it.

In the *Kaṭhōpaniṣad*, seven-year-old Nacikētas asks Yamadēva, the Lord of Death, to teach him about life after death, how a state of deathlessness can be attained. Yamadēva answers Naciketas:

> *śrēyaśca prēyaśca manuṣyamētaḥ...*
>
> Two paths, *śrēyas* (the good) and *prēyas* (the pleasant) approach man... (1.2.2)

The wise one chooses the path of the good, which leads to permanent happiness, whereas the dull-headed one chooses the path of the pleasant, i.e. accumulation and enjoyment, which is impermanent.

The Vēdas do not talk about the good and bad, but about the good and the pleasant, and advises us to transcend both. The Hindu scriptures call the pair of opposites '*dvandva*.' For example,

samaḥ śatrau ca mitrē ca tathā mānāpamānayōḥ
śīta uṣna sukha duḥkhēṣu samaḥ sangavivarjitaḥ

One who is the same to friend and foe, and also in honor and dishonor;
who is the same in cold and heat, and in pleasure and pain (*Bhagavad Gītā*, 12.18)

Lord Kṛṣṇa teaches us that these pairs of opposites are impermanent, and advises us to bear them patiently:

... *āgamāpayinaḥ anityāḥ tāmstitīkṣasva bhārata*

... (these pairs of opposites) have a beginning and an end. They are impermanent in their nature. Bear them patiently, O Arjuna. (2.14)

In many places in the *Bhagavad Gītā*, Lord Kṛṣṇa advises us to go beyond the pairs of opposites:

... *nirdvandō nityasattvasthō*...

... free from the pairs of opposites and ever-balanced... (2.45)

...*nirdvandō hi mahābāhō*...

... free from the pairs of opposites, O mighty-armed one... (5.3)

> *... tē dvandvamōhanirmuktāh.....*
>
> ... these men... freed from the delusion of the pairs of opposites... (7.28)
>
> *The second line of the Guru Stōtram is:*
> *dvandvātītam, gagana sadṛśam*
>
> Guru's nature is beyond dualities, and like the sky (space).

The sky or open space accommodates everything but is affected by nothing.

Towards the end of the same verse,

> *ēkam nityam vimalam acalam*
> *sarvadhī sākṣi bhūtam*
>
> (The Guru is) one, permanent, pure, immovable and the witness of everyone's intellects.

I am witness to all the thoughts and emotions that arise in the mind. For example, I am aware of my sadness. When Amma calls me, I become happy; I am aware of happiness in my mind. When She asks me "Son, do you know the *Dēvī Stōtram?*" I tell Her that I do not. I am aware of ignorance in my mind. When She teaches me, I gain knowledge.

I am that Awareness in which *vidyā* (knowledge) and *avidyā* (ignorance) arise, exist and finally dissolves. That pure consciousness, which is the real 'I,' is always there.

We had earlier discussed the topic of Dēvī being both vidyā and avidyā-svarūpiṇī. In the *Laḷitā Sahasranāma*, there are four other names that indicate Dēvī's nature as being both the pairs of opposites and as being beyond them:

> *Ōm dharma adharma vivarjitayai namaḥ*
>
> I bow down to Dēvī, who transcends both virtue and vice. (255)
>
> *Ōm sad asad rūpa dhāriṇyai namaḥ*
>
> I bow down to Dēvī, who assumes the forms of both being and non-being. (661)
>
> *Ōm bhāva abhāva vivarjitāyai namaḥ*
>
> I bow down to Dēvī, who is beyond both being and non-being. (680)
>
> *Ōm kṣara akṣara ātmikāyai namaḥ*
>
> I bow down to Dēvī, who is in the form of both the perishable and imperishable Self. (757)

When I observe myself, I see that I am both the changing and perishable body-and-mind as well as the changeless and imperishable awareness. Both the changing and changeless aspects in me belong to Dēvī alone.

At night (*rātri*), all forms merge into darkness; everything seems to become non-existent.

When I enter an empty hall and say, "There's nobody here!" I am there to know that there is nobody or nothing (else) here! Even when everything disappears, 'I' (awareness) remains. That pure awareness is Dēvī or Kāḷī, who is ever-existing. Kāḷī is also hailed as '*Śmaśāna Vāsinī,*' one who resides in the graveyard. After death, we say nothing exists, but Kāḷī always exists as pure awareness—caitanyam.

Śiva-śaktyaika-rūpiṇī

"Who is Amma?" This question is answered in countless ways by Amma's devotees, based on their personal experiences.

Why does the infinite divine being assume a form? What is the Avatār's main teaching? The main teaching is how to live the life of an ideal human being, and thus how to relate to the world.

There are three types of human beings: the masculine, the feminine, and one who is neither wholly masculine nor feminine.

In Amma and other divine incarnations, we see a perfect balance of the masculine and the feminine, i.e. *śiva-śaktī-aikyam*, a perfect unity of both. The masculine is considered independent and intellectual, with the head dominating the heart, whereas the feminine is considered dependent and emotional, with the heart dominating the head. A child grows up to become fully developed and mature if he or she has received both the father's disciplining and the mother's loving care and affection.

Modern universities help to develop the heads of youth but not their hearts. This is not so in the āśrams of an ideal Guru. In the *Rāmāyaṇa*, we read about the beautiful āśram of Sage Vasiṣṭha and his wife Arundatī. The sage teaches the scriptures and, when necessary, disciplines his disciples, including Lord Rāma and His brothers. When Arundatī treats the disciples with motherly affection, Vasiṣṭha protests. "You're spoiling them! They are brahmacārīs and should be subjected to a hard and tough life in the āśram."

Arundatī replies, "True, but if there is only disciplining and no love or affection, the disciples will not develop compassion in their hearts."

On completion of their education, Rāma and His brothers return to the palace in Ayōdhyā, where the queen mothers lavish love and attention on them. King Daśaratha protests, "They are no longer children, but grown-up warriors! Don't spoil them!" The queens respond by saying that a mother's love and affection alone can fill the hearts of great warriors with compassion. Devoid of compassion and filled merely with physical strength and skill, they may become Rāvaṇas and Kamsas.[35]

Śrī Śāradā Dēvī, consort of Śrī Rāmakṛṣṇa Paramahamsa, used to give sweets to the brahmacārīs (Swāmi Vivēkānanda and others before they became sanyāsīs). Śrī Rāmakṛṣṇa would object, telling Śāradā Dēvī that She was spoiling them and weakening their austerities and dispassionate attitude. Śāradā Dēvī would counter His argument with the claim that the Guru's strict disciplining is balanced by the love and affection of the *Gurupatnī*, the Guru's spouse.

A few years ago, during Amma's North Indian Tour, the brahmacārīs and brahmacāriṇīs were working hard in the hot sun during one of Amma's Brahmasthānam programs. A devotee asked them, "Can I get you some ice-cream?" When they assented, he got them each a cup of ice-cream.

When Amma learned about this, She asked the brahmacārīs and brahmacāriṇīs, "How could you do such a thing?" She

35 Rāvaṇa was the enemy of Lord Rāma, and Kamsa that of Lord Kṛṣṇa.

scolded all of them and reminded them that they were spiritual seekers. That was the Guru in Amma.

When the tour group reached the next Brahmasthānam temple, Amma announced that She was preparing *pāyasam* (sweet pudding) for all. That was the Gurupatnī in Amma!

There was a small family, comprising a father, mother and two children. The father would often get angry with his children, scold them and even spank them sometimes. The affectionate mother would console her children, and explain to them the cause of their father's anger: a low salary, which made him worry constantly about how he was going to make both ends meet. The mother also encouraged her children to be patient.

Their patience was rewarded: the father received a job-offer in Dubai, one that paid a high salary. After he left for Dubai, the rules changed. The mother felt that she had to be stern with her children, lest they become spoiled in the father's absence. When he came back on leave for a month, the father would be gentle and affectionate with the children, whom he would not have seen for eleven months. Thus, circumstances brought out the father in the mother and vice versa.

Thus, there is a woman in every man and a man in every woman. True education is creating a balance of both in each individual, the balance of head and heart. For Amma, considered response (and not knee-jerk reaction) to any situation is spontaneous; Her heart always supports Her head. She has come to help us grow into fully evolved human beings.

She Came Down to Bring Sītā Back

Amma once told me to cover my head with a cloth, and so I did. A few devotees asked me why She had said so. I said I did not know; when the Guru asks the disciple to do something, the disciple just does it without asking why.

But after many devotees repeatedly asked me why I cover my head with a cloth, I asked Amma why She insists that I cover my head. Amma's reply was vague. After that, I never asked Her again.

However, shortly thereafter, I read an interesting article entitled 'Cloth Caps,' which explained that meditating with the head covered with a cloth is highly beneficial, for the cloth helps to retain the spiritual power generated by meditating. This may be one reason why adherents of certain religions use cloth to cover their heads when they enter their place of worship.

But another reason appealed to me much more. Sanyāsīs of certain monastic orders cover their heads to symbolize the 'feminine attitude' of a sincere seeker approaching the only male, the *Paramātma* (Supreme Self), sometimes known as the *Puruṣa* (Supreme Being).

When Mīrābāī, the great devotee of Lord Kṛṣṇa, wanted to become a sanyāsī, many sanyāsīs objected, saying "Sanyāsa is for males only."

Mīrābāī politely replied, "I know of only one male in this universe, the Puruṣa, and He is the Lord of the gōpīs of Vṛndāvan. All the other living beings in creation are females!"

This is certainly true. Every living being is knowingly or unknowingly moving towards the common goal: union with the Supreme Being. In this spiritual journey, the qualities that can help us are mostly feminine, starting with *jijñāsā* (the intense desire to know God), *śraddhā* (faith), *titīkṣā* (forbearance), *kṣamā* (patience), *karuṇā* or *dayā* (compassion), and the submissive attitude of surrender, generally seen in greater measure in females than in males.

These are the qualities that enable a peaceful and harmonious existence in the universe. We can see in the Purāṇas that every great king who ruled India had all the great qualities in them: the masculine qualities of authority, intelligence and physical strength, and the feminine qualities of humility, patience and compassion. In contrast, the demon kings, powerful though they were, only possessed masculine qualities. In the absence of feminine qualities, they became brutes, causing an imbalance in the natural order in creation. The Supreme Being had to incarnate in order to destroy them.

In Śrī Rāma, Śrī Kṛṣṇa and our beloved Amma, we can see a perfect balance of both male and female qualities, whereas in Rāvaṇa and Kamsa, we can see only an aggressive, masculine force. Even Tāṭakā[36] had to be killed because, even though she had a female body, her nature was masculine.

One of the purposes of the Avatār is to bring about a balance between the masculine and feminine. Lord Rāma's tireless,

---

36 An ogress, reputed to have the strength of a thousand elephants. Lord Rāma killed her in order to protect people who were being terrorized by her.

determined search for the kidnapped Sītā was not that of an infatuated husband trying to reclaim his beautiful wife. Instead, it represents a restoration of all the virtuous qualities that Sītā signifies. We uphold different aspects of the arts such as poetry and music as well as different discoveries in science by honoring the luminaries associated with those accomplishments. For the same reason, we pay homage to Lord Kṛṣṇa because He incarnated to restore *dharma* (righteousness). Human power is limited. When values become corrupt, only a divine power can restore them; ordinary humans cannot.

In this dark age of *Kali,*[37] feminine qualities are fast disappearing—first from men, then from women—causing a serious threat to the very existence of human beings on this planet. It is to restore the 'woman' in the man and the 'woman' in the woman that the Supreme Being incarnated, in the form of a woman, in our midst on September 27th, 1953.

37 According to Hindu cosmogony, every cycle of creation is made up of four yugas (epochs). The Kaliyuga, the fourth and present epoch, is characterized by strife and moral decline.

Ardhanārīśvarī

Amma was due to come down any moment for the morning darśan. Through my window, I saw an American devotee cradling a cute baby in his paternal arms. I stepped out of my room and gazed at the baby briefly. It returned my gaze with wide, innocent, blue eyes. I walked up to the baby and, pretending to be grave like a police officer, extended my hand and said, "Hey Mister, show me your passport and visa!" In response, the baby beamed a beautiful smile, caught hold of my index finger and started chewing it! That was its passport and visa—its purity and innocence!

The proud father said, "Swāmi, it is a Miss, not a Mister!"

I asked the baby, "Are you a Mister or Miss, baby?" Again, the same innocent smile! Neither Miss nor Mister, American nor German nor French. Just blissful existence—*I Am*! We can sense this in Amma also. Scriptures often compare God-realized saints to a child or baby—theirs being a life of simple, joyful existence, devoid of any identification.

When we raise a baby, we don't just feed it with food; we feed it with ideas about identity, conduct, social norms, dos and don'ts, and many other things, thus conditioning it.

When a boy cries out of sadness, he is told, "Dīpak, don't behave like a girl. Be a man!" Or when a girl talks loudly or runs about, she is told "Dīpa, stop acting like a boy. Sit down and be quiet!" In this way, we suppress a child's natural way of expressing emotions, and condition him or her to act according to certain ideas.

When a child is made conscious of its being a boy or a girl for the sake of teaching it morality, discipline and character, it is understandable. But nowadays, there is so much unhealthy competition between the sexes arising from a distorted perception of the relation between the two sexes, prejudices and neuroses arising from gender identity. This competition is on the rise everywhere. There is an increasing demand for "equal rights." Everyone is becoming much more aware of one's rights. But how many realize that rights and responsibilities go hand in hand?

Only a human being wants to become something else. A rose does not want to become a jasmine, nor a jasmine, a lotus. A lion is beautiful in its own way, and so is a peacock. Let us not compare and conclude that one is superior to or better than the other.

A man is great in his own way, and a woman, in her own way. In God's creation, everything is beautiful and has a respectable place in the universe.

For a male spiritual aspirant, attraction to a woman is a great obstacle to the goal, God-realization; for a female spiritual aspirant, attraction to a man is. But it is foolish to belittle or dislike the opposite sex for this reason.

Amma says that there is a man in every woman and a woman in every man. As spiritual aspirants, we should develop those masculine and feminine qualities that will help us advance on the spiritual path. 'Masculine' qualities would include discrimination and dispassion, and 'feminine' qualities would include meekness and total dependence on the Guru. Amma is a blend of all the positive masculine and feminine qualities. That is why we worship Her with the mantra, "*Ōm śiva-śaktyaikya rūpiṇyai namaḥ.*" She is *Ardhanārīśvarī*: half female, half male.

An English professor was listening to a discourse by a *Bhāgavatam* teacher, who would sometimes refer to God as He and at other times as She. The professor asked the teacher, "Is your God a Miss or a Mister?"

The teacher replied, "God is a Mystery!"

Amma has assumed the feminine form. However, during the *Brahmasthāna Pratiṣṭha* (consecration ceremony of the Brahmasthānam Temple), She assumes Śiva Bhāva, the divine demeanor of Lord Śiva. In addition, Amma has a Dēvī Bhāva and a Kṛṣṇa Bhāva. Amma is therefore all three—Miss, Mister and Mystery.

Every one of us was born of a union between man and woman. Our existence can be traced back to a long line of fathers and grandfathers, mothers and grandmothers. Therefore, when a man says, "Women are no good!" isn't he damning the women in his own family? Or, when a woman says, "Men are no good," isn't she insulting her forefathers?

Whatever Śiva can do, his Śaktī can do also. At the time of Dakṣa's yajña,[38] Satī could have destroyed Dakṣa's yajña Herself,

38 Once, when Satī's father, Dakṣa, conducted a yajña, he snubbed Śiva, his son-in-law, by not inviting Him. Not only that, during the yajña itself, he insulted Śiva before all the guests. Unable to bear the insult to Her Lord, Satī jumped into the sacrificial fire and immolated Herself. Śiva's attendants who had accompanied Satī destroyed the yajña and killed Dakṣa.

but She demonstrated the feminine strengths of meekness, steadfastness and unswerving devotion to Her husband Śiva.

Similarly, Sītā could have destroyed Rāvaṇa Herself, who was, apart from Śrī Rāma, one of the most powerful men alive. Rāvaṇa, in fact, finds himself powerless when facing Sītā; he could only threaten Her verbally. Sītā, the Divine Mother, demonstrates the feminine strengths of patience, chastity and utmost loyalty to Her Lord, even in the most trying circumstances. Śrī Rāma, on the other hand, displays the masculine qualities of abidance by dharma, strength and courage.

When a woman tries to become a man, it is because she does not understand the cosmic laws that govern the universe. Only human beings fail to keep pace with the rhythms of the universe.

When Śrī Rāma and Lakṣmaṇa meet the vānaras while searching for Sītā, Sugrīva, one of the vānaras, tells them that he had seen a woman dropping her jewels from an aerial chariot. When he shows them the jewels, Rāma is blinded by tears, and asks Lakṣmaṇa to verify if they are Sītā's jewels. After looking over the jewels, Lakṣamana says, "I cannot recognize the necklace, ear rings or bangles, but these anklets are certainly Sītā's. I recognize them because I see them every day when I prostrate at Her divine feet."

So noble was the culture in India, where the younger brother would regard his elder brother's wife as his mother, and, in that spirit, prostrate before her. Not only that, in some Indian communities, men call both their wives and daughters "Amma" ("mother"). Such is the respect accorded to females. Therefore, it is not true that Indian culture gives women a lower place than men.

Actually, the fact that most cultures have an inherent respect for the feminine is indicated by terms like 'motherland,' 'mother-tongue,' 'mother earth' and 'mother nature.' We also refer to rivers, ships and other objects by the feminine pronoun 'she.'

Nice Person or Good Person?

The first thing that someone walking through the main gates of Amṛtapuri notices is the imposing facade of the Kāḷī Temple. A grand tableau from the *Bhagavad Gītā* of Lord Kṛṣṇa steering Arjuna into war looms large over the temple entrance. On either side of the stairway are ferocious lions guarding the temple.

If the āśram is a haven of peace and compassion, why these iconic representations of aggression? They are symbols of active goodness. They mark the victory of dharma over adharma, the forces of righteousness prevailing over those of unrighteousness.

We celebrate *Dīpāvali*, Christmas and other such festivals commemorating the triumph of goodness over evil. But have we really exterminated evil from our world? Why do evil forces prosper? Because the good forces are inactive; in other words, good for nothing!

Evil forces win because they are convinced that theirs is the right way. Among evil forces, there is loyalty. If not, they know that they will get killed. Evil prevails because virtues such as dedication, unity, conviction, honesty, love and sacrifice are misplaced.

It is better to be a *good* person than a *nice* person, although one should ideally be both. Niceness is often just skin-deep, whereas a good person is responsible, creates peace, or strives to preserve conditions that uphold peace and righteousness.

When we say there is no peace, we mean there is no peace in the human world. If we went on a safari, we would feel the peace in the jungle. It is only in the human world that there are problems. Man's interference is the cause of all problems. There is an ancient Greek saying: "In peace, sons bury their fathers, and in wars, fathers bury their sons."

Once, a teacher asked some students, "Do you prefer peace or war?"

The students replied, "Peace."

"Why?" the teacher asked.

"Because war creates history, and then we have to study for it!" replied the students.

Once, when faced with many problems, a man demanded, "Why is God not doing anything?"

His friend asked, "Why don't you ask God?"

"I did," the first man replied. "And He asked me the same thing: 'Why aren't *you* doing anything about it?'"

Everyone has a responsibility in maintaining peace. All other creatures are controlled by nature, and therefore there is no problem in their world. God has given free will, intelligence and choice only to human beings. These gifts come with the responsibility of using them wisely. However, we misuse these gifts.

A man who has built a house and who has children will realize that it is his responsibility to take care of them. In the same way, we should put our own house in order by first finding peace within ourselves and then radiating it outside.

No man is an island; he is a social animal. The actions of others affect us as much as our actions affect them. When the twin towers in New York collapsed on September 11th, 2001, the whole world was affected. The world is a global village, and all beings are interdependent.

Actually, there is peace within us but we have created disturbances. Once we stop creating the causes of disturbances, peace will be restored.

When Kāḷidās was chopping the very branch on which he was sitting, people laughed at him, calling him a fool. But aren't we doing the same thing? Didn't we create the causes of global warming? Now that we are facing the effects of global warming, we foolishly wonder why.

People often act indiscriminately because they want and care only for quick results. Unfortunately, quick results often have negative effects in the long run, but we are not aware of this.

When the New Year dawns, we wish others, "Happy New Year!" But are we getting what we long for? No. If we work for something, either individually or as a group, shouldn't we get it? We haven't experienced Happy New Years because our notion of happiness is confined to ourselves. We are interested only in making ourselves comfortable. But comfort is not happiness.

Scientists say that birds flying in a V-formation use much less energy when they fly across the ocean. If we want to be happy, we must stop being individualistic.

In India, there is a prayer: "May all beings be kind to me." However, we often fail to understand that if we want others to be kind to us, we must first be kind to them. This is the law of nature. Everyone is subject to this law, even the mightiest dictators.

We often see the rich becoming richer and the poor becoming poorer. Why can't we just take what we want? Suppose there is a store of eatables. If we followed the creed of selfishness, the strong would take everything away, leaving nothing for the weak. But in the end, both will die: the weak by starvation, and the strong by over-eating!

In creation, God created human beings in the spirit of yajña. This is the spirit of joyfully and willingly giving away to others, keeping only what's absolutely necessary for oneself:

> *sahayajñāh prajāh sṛṣṭvā purōvāca prajāpatiḥ*
> *anena prasaviṣyadvamēṣa vōssstvṣṭākāmadhuk*
>
> Having created human beings together with sacrifices at the beginning of creation, the Creator said, "By this shall you prosper. Let this be the milch cow of your desire." (*Bhagavad Gītā*, 3.10)

In the third and fourth chapters of the *Bhagavad Gītā*, Lord Kṛṣṇa nourishes us with the wisdom of the yajña. In the first verse of the fourth chapter, He says that He taught this wisdom at the beginning of creation to Lord Sun, who, in turn, taught it to His son Manu, who taught it to His Son Ikṣvaku, who was the first king of the Solar dynasty in which Lord Rāma was born.

Hindus worship cosmic powers like the sun to offer thanks for the selfless service they render to all living beings. For example, the sun gives light and energy in equal measure to all living beings without partiality. This is a yajña—the spirit of sacrifice, in which one performs actions for the good of the entire world.

During the yajña, the priests offer items like ghee into the fire and pray to be blessed with all that is essential for physical and mental growth. Skeptics might ask, "Why waste precious ghee when there is so much poverty in the world?" The answer is that a pot contains only an equivalent of one teaspoonful of ghee from all the participants. The prayer and attitude of every participant in the yajña is *'Lōkāḥ samastah sukhinō bhavantu.'* Every individual offers what little he or she has and prays for the well-being of all and for universal peace.

In general, people do not have this tendency. Asia has two-thirds of the world's population but only one-third of the world's wealth. Conversely, the West has one-third of the world's population but owns two-third of the world's wealth.

In the *Bhagavad Gītā*, Śrī Kṛṣṇa also says that in the passage of time, the spirit of yajña is lost, and then, He incarnates to restores the lost spirit and glory of the yajña.

The decadence had already set in during Arjuna's time, which was when Kṛṣṇa incarnated to restore the spirit of sacrifice. When Mahābali performed a yajña, he did not havc the right attitude. The Lord incarnated as Vāmana and taught him. Only divine Avatārs can teach us what a true yajña is.

Dānam (charity) is a necessary part of the conclusion of any yajña. This part is unfortunately overlooked in most yajñas that takes place today.

A candidate for the post of police officer was asked, "How would you disperse an unruly mob?"

The candidate replied, "I would go to them with a donation box."

A priest once joked, "At parties, I used to wonder where the poor guys were. At Sunday collection, I used to wonder where the rich folks were!"

The *Caṇḍikā Hōma* that took place in Amma's divine presence was an ideal yajña, which was followed by the launch of many charitable initiatives during Amma's Birthday. The offerings into the fire and the chanting of mantras for universal peace bring about a purification of the atmosphere. Such a yajña is very rare, taking place only once in many thousand years, with the offerings made in the presence of a Satguru like Amma. She is indeed the one who receives all our offerings and blesses us with both the *yajña phalam* (the fruits of the sacrifice) and *yajña prasādam*, i.e. health, wealth, longevity, mental peace and spiritual enlightenment.

FROM FORM TO FORMLESS

From Mūrti Pūjā to Kīrtī Pūjā

Imagine a hall full of noisy people. Someone enters, claps his hands to get their attention, and calls out, "*Ōm namaḥ śivāya!* Please keep quiet!" But no one pays any attention to him.

The elderly people who have come with him walk around, requesting people to maintain some silence. They, too, fail.

At this time, the people standing near the entrance to the hall notice a short, plump and dark woman enter the hall. Her beaming countenance is arresting. In whispers, some ask the people standing near them, "Who's she?" No one knows.

As the woman makes her way into the hall, she catches the attention of more and more people, all of whom spontaneously fall into a respectful hush. The only sounds now are of people murmuring. Within moments, pin-drop silence pervades the hall. All eyes are on this woman.

Such is the charisma of a being like Amma. Her mere presence is enough to quieten the hubbub of worldliness. This phenomenon encapsulates, in a nutshell, the effect that a divine being naturally creates in the world by Her mere presence.

The Avatār enters our world silently. It is said that Amma came out of Damayantī-amma's womb silently, without crying.

The sun rises silently and illumines the entire world, which wakes up to activity. Those who chant the Gāyatrī mantra or do the *Sūrya Namaskār* (yōgic exercises) tune their body and mind to receive more of the sun's light and its nourishing rays. The sun does not give more of itself to some or less to others. It nourishes all impartially, and then sets silently.

Śrī Rāma was born into the Solar Dynasty (*Sūrya Vamśa*). He, too, came into the world silently, walked silently though the forests, until He reached the southernmost tip of India, from where he traveled to Śrī Lanka. The elimination of the demonic forces was child's play to Him. He integrated the entire human race into one whole. Many different beings, not just humans, came together as one universal family to witness His coronation. Such is the theme, too, of Amma's mission—Embracing the World.

When Lord Rāma went to the forest, all the citizens of Ayōdhyā ran after Him. When Śrī Kṛṣṇa left Vṛndāvan, all the denizens of the village ran after Him. When Amma leaves Amṛtapuri for any program, in India or outside, one can witness a similar phenomenon—Her children running, seemingly without brakes, after Amma! How many CEOs have this effect on their employees?

This is one reason why Rāma, Kṛṣṇa and Amma are all hailed by the epithet 'Kṛṣṇa.' One meaning of 'Kṛṣṇa' is 'One who has the power of attraction.'

The nature of their attractiveness is different from that of worldly attractions, which are like fireworks. Their explosions and bright colors are dazzling. Hardly anyone notices the moon in the background, silently illumining the night sky with its soothing rays. The fireworks stay for a few minutes and then disappear, whereas the moonlight is silent and constant.

Worldly accomplishments or personalities are often like fireworks. They make their entrances on the world's stage and disappear into oblivion shortly. The spiritual master and the Avatār are, in contrast, like the moon—silent and permanent. They take us to the goal of human life, to the state of Supreme Consciousness.

Lord Kṛṣṇa was born into the Lunar Dynasty (*Candra Vamśa*). His enchanting form and divine play captivated the women and men of Gōkul alike. When His form had become deeply impressed in the hearts of the gōpīs and *gōpas* (cowherds), Kṛṣṇa quietly left for Mathura. From then on, they meditated on Him in their hearts and realized His presence within themselves as Infinite Peace and Blissful Awareness.

Even in the Hindu tradition, there are many who do not accept a God with form. But in the 12th chapter of the *Bhagavad Gītā*, Lord Kṛṣṇa advises Arjuna, "O Arjuna, for you, worship of God with form is ideal." Arjuna represents all of us who have devotion but are unable to conceive of the infinite, formless reality.

In this chapter, Lord Kṛṣṇa says that meditation on the formless infinite is the highest form of meditation. Then comes meditation on the cosmic form. If that is also difficult, we may choose any one form of God, and meditate on it. Most of us are at this level—meditation on one form.

Worship of the divine with form is *mūrti pūjā*. All devotees begin with it. When we understand that every form we see in the universe is a carrier of the divine, our worship becomes elevated to the worship of the divine glory (*kīrtī*) manifest in lesser or greater degrees in everyone and everything. Thus mūrti pūjā becomes kīrtī pūjā.

Some devotees may find it hard to conceive of Amma or their iṣṭa-dēvatā being omnipresent. It doesn't help either that in Indian religious movies, deities are usually seen vanishing from their abode in order to appear where a devotee needs His help! The truth behind such depictions is that God can manifest Himself anywhere He wants.

Both Swāmi Amṛtaswarupānanda and Swāmi Amṛtātmānanda have been blessed to see Amma in flesh and blood when they were away from Amṛtapuri and intensely longing for Her. For Swāmiji, it was in the U.S. that Amma materialized before him in 1987, when he had gone there to prepare for Amma's First World Tour. Swāmi Amṛtātmānanda saw Her in the Himalayas, where he had been wandering for a few months. When Amma manifested in those locations, She was not recorded as having disappeared from Amṛtapuri!

When we were growing up, my younger brother and I had the hobby of rearing domestic fish such as angelfish and goldfish. We had two or three fish tanks, which we kept in our rooms, because we did not want our grandfather, of whom we were in awe, to see them. In our room, we would spend a long time gazing at the fish, and when we were leaving, we would push the fish tanks under our beds so that no one would see them.

Everything went well for some time. One day, one of the fish committed suicide by jumping out of the fish tank! Grandfather, who would come into our room daily to adorn with flowers the pictures of deities, noticed a trail of ants below our beds. We were caught! He ordered us to take out the fish tanks, and chastised us for imprisoning the fish. Having gone to jail with Gāndhiji during India's freedom fight, Grandfather had become sensitive to all forms of incarceration.

He told us to carry the tanks to the lake near the house and wade into it waist-deep. Grandfather then told us to immerse the tanks in the water. For some time, the fish continued swimming inside the tank. After that, one by one, the fish came out and were free.

After meeting Amma and joining Her āśram, I have come to realize that many people are like fish in a tank. Family life is akin to a fish tank. We should come out of the fish tank of our families, and enjoy swimming in the ocean of the universal family. Anyone who has seen Amma or visited Her in Amṛtapuri or any other place She visits would have understood what it means to be a part of much larger community, bound by ties of love and affection.

May Amma inspire us all to a life of serving and loving others, seeing in others the divine consciousness that shines in all alike.

Seeking and Finding Within

"This is our elephant god!"

This was how a tourist guide in India introduced Lord Gaṇēśa to a tourist, who asked, "Why do Indians worship animals?" The guide had no reply.

Vināyaka or *Gaṇēśa Caturthi* is one of the most popular festivals of India. Those who have seen a baby elephant know how cute it looks. A human baby is even cuter. Even though an elephant's head on a plump human baby might strike some as odd, Lord Gaṇēśa looks adorable! He has inspired countless artists and scultptors to reproduce His image.

The *Gaṇēśa Nāmāvali* (sacred litany of names associated with Lord Gaṇēśa) begins with '*Ōm sumukhāya namaḥ*'—'I bow down to Him with a beautiful face!'

Gaṇēśa is *buddhi-dātā*, one who bestows knowledge; hence, the big head. When asked to circumambulate the world, Gaṇēśa went around His divine parents Śiva and Pārvatī, indicating that they alone created the whole universe. As children of Amma, we know that gaining Amma is as good as gaining the entire world, and losing Her is as good as losing the entire world. Amma is everything for us!

Lord Gaṇēśa taught Kubēra, the God of Wealth, a lesson in humility and wisdom. Kubēra had imagined that since Lord Śiva was always meditating and His consort Pārvatī always sitting beside Him, Gaṇēśa and his brother Muruga were not getting enough to eat! He decided to show off his wealth. Kubēra invited

Lord Gaṇēśa to his palace for a feast, not realizing what he would be in for! Gaṇēśa ate everything, including the vessels, and said that He was still hungry. He threatened to swallow Kubēra if he did not sate His hunger fully. Kubēra ran to Kailāś, and fell at the feet of Gaṇēśa's divine parents. Gaṇēśa ran after him. Pārvatī, who is also Annapūrṇēśvarī, the Goddess of Nourishment, fed Her son a handful of puffed rice. Gaṇēśa became satisfied at once!

The symbolic meaning of this story is that human beings will never be satisfied, no matter how much they learn or no matter how much they acquire. But just a little spiritual sustenance leads one to becoming *tṛptaḥ*—satisfied or content. Gaṇēśa is called Kumbōdhara, which means 'pot-bellied.' This, too, signifies *tṛpti*: "I am full and complete, and there is nothing more to be attained!"

Devotees often debate whether God has form or not. A systematic study of the scriptures helps us understand that God is both with form and formless. One cannot see hydrogen and oxygen in their gaseous state, but when they become water vapor, we can see it. When vapor becomes water, we can feel it. When water becomes ice, we can hold it. The word 'Avatār' means 'coming down' from the highest, subtlest state to the lowest, grossest state, which can be known by sense organs.

God has form. In fact, all forms in this universe are God's. We choose a form that we find ideal for worshipping, but we must remember that this is just one form that the Supreme Being has assumed. The *Gaṇapati Atharva Śīrṣam* declares, "You are Brahma, Viṣṇu, Śiva! You are Indra! You are Vāyu! You are Sūrya!

You are Candra!" There is a similar mantra in the *Nārāyaṇa Upaniṣad*, "Nārāyaṇa is everything!" In the *Dēvī Atharva Śīrṣam*, it is said that Dēvī alone appears in the form of all the gods and other inferior living beings. So, too, in *Śrī Rudram*, there is a mantra that states that Rudra (Śiva) is the Lord of every being in the universe. In other words, it is the Formless alone that appears as the countless forms in this universe.

During *Gaṇēśa Caturthi*, devotees worship Lord Gaṇēśa's form for many days and finally immerse the idol in the ocean, which represents the infinite being. This ritual symbolizes the form merging into the formless.

Amma, the Guru, is the bridge between the form and the formless. From Her form (*rūpam*), She takes us to Her real nature (*svarūpam*).

Śrī Rāma constructed more than one bridge. He brought Daśaratha's and Janaka's kingdom together. Daśaratha was a worshipper of God with form. Janaka meditated on the formless, Supreme Being. The unity of Daśaratha and Janaka shows the harmony between meditation on form and worship of the formless.

The Vaiṣṇavites (devotees of Lord Viṣṇu and His Avatārs) worship God with form. The Śaivites (devotees of Lord Śiva) regard the Supreme as formless. By worshipping the Śiva linga in Rāmēśvaram, Lord Rāma, an incarnation of Viṣṇu, brought the Vaiṣṇavites and Śaivites together.

Similarly, Swāmi Ayyappa is the son of Ayya (Viṣṇu) and Appa (Śiva); it signifies the coming together of meditation on

God with and without form. When we go to Śabarimala, the earthly abode of Lord Ayyappa, we first worship Ayyappa with form, and conclude by worshipping *Makara-jyōtī*,[39] the formless. How wonderful our culture is and how enlightened our spiritual masters are!

Similarly, devotees of Amma first worship Her in the form that we see before us. Gradually, we become aware that we see, smell, hear, touch and feel because of Her divine presence within us. We then experience Amma's presence within us as infinite peace, joy and compassion.

In the bhajan '*Prabhō Gaṇapatē*,' we sing the following lines,

> *tēḍi tēḍi engō ōḍungiṇḍrār - unnai*
> *tēḍi kaṇḍu koḷḷalāmē*
>
> People run around in the hope of finding You.

If we substitute the word '*unnai*' with '*uḷḷam*' ('heart'), the lines mean 'People run around, and can find You in the heart.'

---

39 The star that appears when the sun transits in Capricorn (makara), usually on January 14th. Devotees believe that the celestial lighting that takes place on this day is a manifestation of Lord Ayyappa.

Vyōmavat Vyāpta Dēhāya

In Amṛtapuri, at the start of the scriptural classes, we chant

> *vyōmavat vyāpta dēhāya*
> *dakṣināmūrtayē namaḥ*
>
> I bow down to Guru Dakṣinamūrti Śiva, whose body is as expansive (infinite) as space.

Similarly, the *Guru Stōtram* pays hōmage to the Guru who is

> *caitanya śāśvataḥ śantō*
> *vyōmātītō nirañjanaḥ*
>
> ... eternal consciousness, which is of the nature of peace, who transcends space, and who is taintless.

When we worship any form of God, we are trained to lift our minds slowly from the *rūpam* (form) to the *svarūpam* (real nature) of the divinity we worship.

"Why does Mother Kāḷī not wear clothes?" is a question some ask. Kāḷī's effulgent form is either *nīla-varṇa*, blue, or *kṛṣṇa-varṇa*, black. The sky is blue in the day and black at night. The absence of clothes symbolizes Her infinite nature, which cannot be contained in any way. She is the Supreme Being from whom the entire creation comes into existence and finally dissolves. Even space comes into existence from Her.

Mother Kāḷī's uncovered breasts dispense the divine milk of *bhukti*, worldly prosperity, and *mukti*, spiritual liberation. Hence,

She is hailed as *bhukti-mukti-pradātrī*, one who bestows bhukti and mukti.

Mother Kāḷī wears a garland of human heads. The head signifies the power of knowledge. The garland thus indicates that all knowledge is Hers. Kāḷī also wears a skirt of human hands. Hands symbolize actions and power. Therefore it indicates that all power to act comes from Her alone!

Some ask why Kāḷī drinks blood. Blood represents energy and strength. People take pride in their strength. The drinking of blood is a symbolic representation reminding us that all energy (*śaktī*) belong to Her. Kumkum is red in color, and it represents the blood and energy in each one of us. When we daub kumkum on our foreheads, let us do it with the remembrance that the power with which we do all actions is divine, and therefore, let us strive to use this power to do only good and noble deeds.

Many devotees of Amma wear necklaces with lockets featuring a picture of Amma's face or Her feet. This pendant rests close to our hearts, thus fostering devotion for Amma. We might wear rings with Amma's photo. May they remind us to remember Her in all our actions.

Many years ago, when we accompanied Amma to the famous Mūkāmbikā temple, eight priests carrying the *pūrṇakumbha*[40] came forward to the main entrance to receive Amma with all reverence.

Offering the pūrṇakumbha to the Guru is significant for two reasons:

---

40 Vessel filled with water, usually offered to welcome the Guru.

1. the fullness of the pūrṇakumbha represents the devotion-filled hearts of the disciple or devotee. In other words, we should receive or approach the Guru with utmost devotion.
2. the pūrṇakumbha represents the Guru's real nature, which is characterized by fullness, wholeness or infinitude.

When we offer the pūrṇakumbha to our Guru, we are not reminding Amma of Her true nature, of course! Amma does not forget Her real nature even for a second! It is we who forget Her nature, just like Arjuna forgot Lord Kṛṣṇa's divinity. Therefore, the pūrṇakumbha reminds us about Her infinite nature, and is a humble prayer to Her to reveal our true, infinite nature to us:

antaḥ pūrṇō bahiḥ pūrṇō
pūrṇakumbha ivārṇavē
antaḥ śūnyō bahiḥ śūnyō
śūnyakumbha ivāmbarē
pūrṇāya sadguravē namaḥ
pūrṇakumbham samarpayāmi

I offer the pūrṇakumbha to my Satguru, who is infinite in nature, just as a water-pot immersed in an ocean is full of water inside and surrounded totally by water outside, or just as a water-pot in space is empty inside and enveloped in emptiness.

The *Bhagavad Gītā* compares the God-realized sage to an ocean that is full, but which never overflows even when all the rivers in the world flow into it. Amma is like this ocean.

Is it possible for an ordinary human being to sit continuously for 18 hours, hugging up to 48,000 devotees, mostly with just Her right hand? (A person working in an office from 9 a.m. to 5 p.m. usually takes at least a couple of breaks.) The problems and grievances that the devotees unburden upon Amma during darśan are enough to drive a psychiatrist crazy. While giving darśan, Amma is consulted by people holding responsibilities in Her institutions and who need answers to queries. Amidst this swirl of activities, a family of eight comes to Amma for blessings. Amma puts candies in the mouths of seven of them; to the eighth, She offers a tiny piece, for She remembers that he is diabetic!

Such is the real nature of our Guru. Amma's awareness is not limited to Her individual self, but is all-pervading. She has awareness both of the inside and the outside. She knows that the whole universe consisting of names and forms is nothing but a play of infinite consciousness. The never-ending variety of names and forms does not exist for Her, who sees only the same divinity everywhere.

Watchwoman

There was a great Sufi saint named Baal Shem. He would go to the seashore late every night and sit there for hours in deep meditation. A night watchman noticed this. One day, he asked Baal Shem, "Sir, why do you do this every night?"

Baal Shem asked the watchman, "Why do you stay awake at night?"

The watchman replied, "I'm a night watchman."

Baal Shem replied "So am I. I'm also a watchman."

The surprised watchman asked, "But, sir, what do you watch, sitting with your eyes closed?"

Baal Shem replied, "You watch and keep away thieves. I watch thieves like anger, jealousy and lust within me, and the most dangerous thief called the mind or ego."

The mind or ego steals joy, peace and contentment. How can we get rid of these thieves once and for all? Call on the Thief who is on the lookout for these thieves. Yes, there is a thief who steals the dangerous mind!

citta-cōra yaśōda kē bāl
navanīta cōra gōpāl!

Stealer of the mind, Mother Yaśōda's child,
Stealer of butter, Cowherd boy.

Lord Kṛṣṇa steals our minds; He is *citta-cōra*. He steals butter, too, i.e. our attachments, the feeling that something belongs to us. Everything belongs to God. He is in each one of us, and gives us the power to think, speak and act. He is called *'antaryāmi'* – One who remains inside (our hearts) and controls us.

One of the mantras in the *Laḷitā Sahasranāma* is *'Sadā-ācāra-pravartikā'* (356), which means 'She who makes us perform good actions and cultivate good habits.' Some of our āśram swāmis gave it another meaning based on their experiences with Amma; they twisted the name – *'Sadā-cāra-pravartikā'* – 'One who spies on us!' (In Malayalam, *'cāra'* means 'spy.') That is exactly what Amma does. She might be thousands of miles away in USA, but knows what is in the minds of each one of us, wherever we may be. Such is the experience of thousands of devotees.

Amma watches not only our actions and words but our thoughts as well. In Her divine presence, we slowly learn to entertain only pure and positive thoughts, which give us a strong, healthy, calm and peaceful mind.

We could well say that Amṛtapuri manufactures the best 'watches.'

- W - Words
- A - Actions
- T - Thoughts
- C - Characters
- H - Habits

Like Baal Shem, Amma is a watch(wo)man. In addition, She is also a watch manufacturer and watch repairer. Of what use is a beautiful wristwatch, one studded with gems, which does not show the correct time? Of what use is a human being who has intelligence, good looks, skill and strength but no character? Such a person is like Rāvaṇa.

At the end of the *Mahābhārata*, the five Pāṇḍavas begin their ascent to heaven, climbing a treacherous mountain. One by one, they begin to fall and perish:

- Sahadēva, the most intelligent;
- Nakula, the most handsome;
- Arjuna, the most skilful; and
- Bhīma, the strongest.

Only Yudhiṣṭhira, the good and dharmic person, remains, eventually ascending to heaven. The story has a deep, symbolic meaning. One's intelligence, beauty, skill and strength will disappear towards the end of one's life, whereas one's character and goodness will remain and raise one to divinity, to eternity.

The Watchwoman is *always* watching us. Let us surrender our Words, Actions, Thoughts, Character and Habits to Amma. She will purify us and make us worthy of, and useful to, our families, society, country and the entire world.

Amṛtam Dēhi

One question that may arise in our minds is: "Have we *really* known Amma by now?" Every opportunity to know Amma has only led us to greater and greater wonder and reverence. Or, how can we, from our level, really know the Mother of the Universe and explain the purpose of Her present incarnation?

The original face of the āśram has changed substantially over the years; so, too, Amma's approach. How strict and stern She used to be years ago! Eight hours of meditation for all āśram residents; frugal food; taking only the minimum needed to sustain the body... In those days of austerities, Amma, our Guru and God, was especially vigilant about our spiritual progress. She was our sole refuge and inspiration on the spiritual path.

Amma is aware of our every thought, word and deed. This is what my numerous experiences prove unmistakably, and this has only increased my reverence and devotion towards Her over the years. Therefore, I am usually subdued in Her presence.

Many years ago, Amma entrusted me with the responsibility of teaching Vēdānta in the āśram. I took it up gladly, thinking that doing so would make my life meaningful by allowing me to share what I had learned with others. Once, when Amma went abroad, She asked me to conduct two classes daily, one for the seniors and another for juniors. In the beginning, I had no problem. But gradually, the classes became burdensome. I had to spend most of my time preparing for them, leaving me with no time to do my regular sādhana, which included japa, dhyāna and arcana. I became greatly anxious and perturbed.

At that time, a swāmi who had been traveling with Amma returned to Amṛtapuri. He brought me a letter from Amma. I eagerly opened it and saw a two-line message: "Son, you are now feeling stressed because you are not able to continue your sādhana, aren't you? You need to teach only one class a day."

Amma needs no time to read our minds or prescribe remedies for our problems. She also tests Her children according to their capacity of endurance. Any Satguru, who desires the uplift of the disciple, will be like that.

Before meeting Amma, I was studying Vēdānta in another āśram. There, one could study the scriptural texts by attending regular classes, but opportunities for clearing doubts were inadequate. It was then that I had the great blessing of meeting Amma. During the first darśan itself, Amma cleared all my doubts, one after the other, without my saying anything. In those moments, I became aware of my mental burdens vanishing, some simplicity and peace dawning in my mind, and my being transformed into a small and innocent child in Amma's loving hands.

I asked Amma if I could join Her āśram. My goal in life then had been to gain a vision of Goddess Durgā. When I saw Amma's Bhāva darśan, I felt that my wish had been fulfilled!

Amma said, "Complete the Vēdānta course, serve that āśram for some time in return for the knowledge gained, get the permission of and blessings from the resident *ācārya* to leave, and then inform Amma."

After completing the Vēdānta course, the ācārya asked me about my future plans. I told him about my aspirations. He readily gave me his permission to join Amma's āśram, and blessed me, saying, "*Jagadambē śaraṇam! Jagadambē śaraṇam!*" – "I take refuge in the Mother of the Universe!"

I wrote to Amma and waited. Meanwhile, being aware of the discipline in Amma's āśram, I engaged myself in rigorous sādhana. My only goal was to gain the vision of Goddess Durgā. I wrote, not one or two, but seven letters to Amma but did not get any response. I began worrying. My tapas began flagging. Anxiety, disappointment and excessive eating undermined my sādhana. I vacillated between hope and despair.

Then, like a beam of immortal love piercing the heart of spiritual darkness, Amma's reply came, a two-line letter: "Son, you are neglecting your sādhana. You have lost your self-control. Wait until Amma calls you. Do not worry. Amma is with you!"

From then on, I never looked back. Amma is always with me. This is not my experience alone. Many devotees have had similar experiences. I have had the good fortune of witnessing some such instances.

Once, while traveling with Amma, we were passing through a small suburb of Kōṭṭayam, Kēraḷa, at about 10 p.m. when Amma suddenly started exclaiming loudly, "I want *vaḍa* (a fried snack)! I want vaḍa!"

No shop was open so late at night. Amma continued demanding vaḍas. When our efforts to find vaḍas failed, Amma asked the driver to take the vehicle to Kākkanāḍ. The moment we reached there, Amma asked the driver to stop. She then got down and rushed into a private residence. There, in the kitchen, a woman was chanting her mantra and making vaḍas. Amma entered the kitchen and started eating the hot vaḍas. That devotee was struck by awe and wonder, and tears of joy flowed profusely from her eyes.

On another occasion, a family was waiting expectantly for Amma at home, which had been decorated in a simple yet elegant manner. The woman of the house had kept a container of yogurt in the refrigerator, and instructed everyone in the house not to touch it; she explained that it had been specially prepared for Amma. After a while, Amma arrived, went straight to the kitchen, not to the pūjā room, opened the fridge, took the yogurt and drank some of it.

These two instances show how eager Amma is to bring joy and fulfillment into the lives of Her children. To do this, Amma comes down to their level to bless them. At the same time, She gives them silent hints that She knows all their thoughts, words and actions. These hints strengthen and deepen their faith and devotion.

Once, while traveling by train from Delhi to Kolkata, I began to feel intensely hungry in the evening. It was a Thursday, the day I fast from sunrise to sunset. After 6:30 p.m., I ate some deep-fried snacks served in the train, as nothing else was available. I felt uneasy after eating the oily food, and was thinking seriously of getting some medical help for indigestion. At that time, Amma was giving darśan to the āśram residents traveling with Her. She was distributing *pēḍa* (an Indian confectionery) to everyone. Given how queasy my tummy was feeling, I didn't think I could digest the pēḍa. I was last in the line of people waiting to receive the prasād from Amma. She gave pēḍa to everyone in the line, including the brahmacārī right in front of me. When my turn came, Amma closed the pēḍa container and kept it aside. She then took some grapes from another container and gave that to me. Grapes are easily digestible; they also aid digestion.

Before meeting Amma, I used to keep Her picture before me, compose bhajans and sing them. I did not know Amma's name then. I had only heard someone say "*Vaḷḷikkāvil Amma*" ("Mother from Vaḷḷikkāvu"). One of the bhajans I composed then began like this: "*Amṛtam dēhi, Hanumānē...*" – "Give me immortality, O Hanumān..." Unknowingly, the word '*Amṛtam*' had entered uncannily into the bhajan. If not Amma's *sankalpa* (divine resolve), what else was it? From that day onwards, Amma gave me a clear picture of my goal. This conviction has been proved again and again by every experience thereafter. So it is that I continue singing even today: "*Amṛtam dēhi amṛtēśvarī!*" – "Give me immortality, O Amṛtēśvarī!"

Dr. Śyāmsundar, MBBS.

Once, a pundit in the court of Emperor Akbar[41] narrated the episode known as *Gajēndra Mōkṣa* (Liberation of Gajēndra) from the *Bhāgavatam*. Gajēndra was a great king and devotee of Lord Viṣṇu. As a result of being disrespectful towards a sage, he was cursed to be reborn as an elephant. As an elephant, Gajēndra was bathing in a river when a crocodile (who was a *gandharva* (heavenly being) cursed to be reborn as a reptile) caught hold of one of Gajēndra's legs. Gajēndra struggled to free himself but failed. As a last measure, he plucked a lotus from the river, mentally offered it to Lord Viṣṇu, and prayed to Him for deliverance. The Lord answered his prayer by coming down to earth on His mount, killing the crocodile and saving Gajēndra, thus liberating both crocodile and elephant.

When Akbar heard this story, he laughed and said that there had been no need for Viṣṇu Himself to come to Gajēndra's rescue; He could have sent one of His servants instead. His wise minister Bīrbal said, "O Emperor, give me a little time and I will prove that the Lord's actions were quite natural!"

Bīrbal then had a wax statue made of Prince Sālim, Akbar's favorite son. One morning, when Akbar was standing on his balcony, Bīrbal threw the wax statue of Prince Sālim into the swimming pool and shouted, "Help! Help! Prince Sālim has fallen into the water!"

41 A Mogul dynasty emperor (1556 – 1605 CE).

When Akbar heard this, he dived into the water and brought the wax statue out of the water. When he realized that somebody had played a joke on him, he became very angry and asked who had done so. With folded hands, Bīrbal humbly said, "O Emperor, it was I who arranged this drama. But tell me, when so many of your soldiers are here, why did *you* jump into the water?"

Akbar angrily retorted, "Because Sālim is *my son*!"

Bīrbal calmly replied, "Yes, Emperor. So, too, every being in this universe is God's child, especially those who constantly worship Him!"

God assumes a form and incarnates on earth to remind His creation that they are heirs to infinite joy, and thus inspires them to return to their true abode.

On another occasion, a merchant visiting Akbar's court began praising the emperor to the skies. He said that Akbar was greater than God even. Not one to suffer fools gladly, Akbar asked how that was so. None of his ministers dared to say anything, but witty Bīrbal responded, "Yes, Emperor, the merchant is right, because there's one thing you can do that God cannot!"

"What's that?" asked Akbar.

"God cannot banish anybody from His kingdom, because the whole universe is His kingdom. But you can do it easily!" answered Bīrbal.

In the *Rāmcaritmanas*, the poet praises Lord Rāma thus:

ajānubhuja śaracāpadhara
sangrāma jita kharadūṣaṇam

> Lord Rāma is long-armed, wielding the bows and arrows with His shapely arms, and easily defeated Khara and Dūṣana in battle.

Long arms symbolize beauty and strength, but they also imply arms long enough to embrace the world. Amma is also popular for 'Embracing the World,' the name of Her global mission. None can step out of Her spiritual empire!

Khara and Dūṣana were Rāvaṇa's security force. They would not allow anyone to enter Rāvaṇa's 'territory.' But Lord Rāma made them realize that the entire universe belongs to God and not to any other individual.

A spider weaves a web inside a room and thinks the web its private home! We are also experts in confining ourselves. We think, "This is mine, and what lies beyond this boundary is not!" We are concerned with keeping our house clean but not with environmental cleanliness; hence the need for signs in public places reminding us, "Please do not throw litter here."

In contrast, when Amma launched the Amala Bhāratam Campaign (ABC), She expressed concern for maintaining cleanliness everywhere. (As a spiritual master, She is also an advocate for inner purity.) Behind the campaign is a plea to become more expansive and not to become blindly attached to whatever we think and call 'mine'—my house, my car, my family, my dog!

The ancient sages were aware of this problem:

> *kāntā imē mē, tanayā imē mē*
> *gṛhā imē mē, paśavastu imē mē,*

ēvam narō mēśa samāna rūpaḥ
mē! mē! kṛtaḥ, kāla vṛkēṇa nītaḥ

This is my wife and this is my son.
This is my house, and these, my animals.
Thus man behaves like a goat,
Crying "My! My!" and is finally devoured by the wolf of Time!

Even the most intelligent human being suffers from this problem, which is more serious than any other disease. The wise call it "*bhava rōgaḥ*"—the ailment of worldly existence. One could simply call it "attachment and delusion." The only doctor who can cure this is Dr. Śyāmsundar, MBBS (**M***adhur* **B***ānsurī* **B***hajanēwālā* **Ś***yām*—the dusky divinity who plays the sweetest devotional melodies on His flute).

Every human relationship, place and object gives us a mixture of joy and sorrow—*duḥkha miśrita sukham*, i.e. joy tainted by sorrow. None except the Lord can give us only untainted joy. It was said of Kṛṣṇa, "*mathurādipatē akhilam madhuram*"—"everything about the Lord of Mathura is sweet!"

Recently, some people commented that the present world is so noisy that if Lord Kṛṣṇa were to appear and play His flute, nobody would hear it; He might have to play the *nādasvaram*[42] or saxophone instead! But our spiritual masters say that this is not true. Those who are eager to hear the divine melody can still hear Lord Kṛṣṇa's sweet flute. They will hear it even when

42 An Indian reed instrument, often played in temples; similar to the clarinet.

it is very noisy, whereas those who are distracted will fail to hear even a nādasvaram or saxophone!

When Kṛṣṇa played the flute, not only the gōpīs and gōpas but the cows and calves would also come running. The Lord's flute issues a clarion call to "return home, children!" In His divine presence, all attachments and delusions disappear like clouds dissipated by the bright sun of knowledge! Nothing can drown out the divine flute, which removes all impure thoughts and selfish desires.

We must become like a flute in Kṛṣṇa's hands, i.e. hollow and therefore capable of bringing out sacred music. Like the flute, the cranium has seven holes—the two eyes, two ears, two nostrils and the mouth. If these seats of the senses are totally receptive to Kṛṣṇa, then we become His flute, and the best comes out of us. Kṛṣṇa is called Hṛṣikēśa, which means 'Lord of the senses.'

SOME TEACHINGS

Teachings from the Bhagavad Gītā

Gangā, Gītā and Gāyatrī[43]—these are three of the Divine Mothers who purify us, their children. Among the three, *ācāryas* give first place to the *Bhagavad Gītā*.

In order to be purified by Gangā, we must travel to where the river flows. The Gāyatrī mantra cannot be chanted loudly and it purifies only the one who chants it. But the *Bhagavad Gītā* purifies not only those who chant it but also those who listen to the chanting.

It is said that "*sarva śastramayī gītā*"—the *Gītā* contains the essence of the teachings of all the Vēdas.

The ācāryas advise us, "Don't say, 'I have gone through the *Gītā*.' Ask rather, 'Has the *Gītā* gone through me?'" In other words, we must thoroughly assimilate the teachings of the *Gītā*. Don't say, "I have learned the *Gītā* by heart." Say instead, "I have understood the *Gītā* with my heart." The *Gītā* is a sacred song, and a song can never be understood by the head, only the heart. That is why Lord Kṛṣṇa tells Arjuna, "*Bhaktōऽsi mē sakhā cēti!*"—"You are My devotee and friend" (4.3), and because of this bond of love and trust between them, Kṛṣṇa is ready to teach him. Lord Kṛṣṇa also says in the *Gītā*, "*Śraddhāvān labhatē jñānam*"—"One who has faith gains knowledge" (4.39). Faith is yet another quality of the heart.

43 Gangā is the Ganges River. Gītā refers to the Bhagavad Gītā. Gāyatrī refers to the sacred Gāyatrī mantra. Hindus regard all three as Divine Mothers.

The *Bhagavad Gītā* contains 18 chapters. They teach that every one of us is divine by nature. Our real nature is pure consciousness. We believe that man is body that contains a soul. But the *Gītā* reveals that man is a soul clothed by a body. The 18 chapters explain the sacred mantra *'Tat tvam asi'*—You are That (Supreme Being). The first six chapters explain the *'tvam'* principle, or the individual being, the *jivātma.* The next six chapters explain *'tat,'* or the Supreme Being, the *paramātma.* The last six chapters explain *'asi,'* how the individual becomes one with the Supreme being, just as a drop of water falling into the ocean becomes one with it.

What is the teaching of the *Bhagavad Gītā?* It begins with the word *'dharma'* (*'dharmakṣētrē kurukṣētrē…'*) and ends with the word *'mama'* (*'dhruva nītir matir mama'*). The first and the last words form *'dharma mama'* or *'mama dharma,'* which means 'my duty'—in other words, the performance of one's duties, remembering one's role in the family, society and the country, and, lastly, as a human being.

Usually, we face two problems:

1. Ignorance of what should be done;
2. And if one knows, we generally do not have the strength to do what should be done.

The *Bhagavad Gītā* gives us the clarity of vision (knowledge), purity of mind (devotion and surrender to God), and the strength to perform actions to the best of one's ability.

The main teaching of the *Bhagavad Gītā* can be summed up in a few words, which Lord Kṛṣṇa told Arjuna: "*Mām anusmara yudhya ca*"—"Remember Me and fight" (8.7). What this means is that one must remember God before doing any action, and with the attitude that one is only an instrument in the hands of the Lord.

Here, 'fight' means 'perform one's duties.' Arjuna was a warrior, and his duty was to fight. '*Kuru*' means 'action' and '*kṣētra*' means 'field;' thus, 'Kurukṣētra' refers to the 'field of action,' or one's field of work in daily life.

The vignette of Arjuna seated in the chariot steered by Lord Kṛṣṇa, the charioteer, is symbolic. The chariot represents the human body, and the five horses, the five senses—eyes, ears, nose, tongue and touch. The reins represent the different thoughts that the senses stimulate, and Lord Kṛṣṇa represents the intellect that has assimilated the Vēdic teachings. When the intellect (charioteer) controls the (reins of the) thoughts led by (the horses of) our senses, the (chariot of the) human body reaches its destination, overcoming all obstacles. What is the destination? The Supreme.

What result do we get if we practice the teachings of the *Bhagavad Gītā*? The Lord's teachings begin with the word '*aśōcyān*' ("*Aśōcyān anvaśōcastvam…*") (2.11), which means "Do not grieve." His teachings conclude with the two words "*Mā śucah*"—"Do not grieve." Therefore, the divine teachings take us beyond all sorrow. This sacred teaching was given to Arjuna, a qualified student, and Sage Vyāsa bequeathed it to the world through 700 verses.

The *Bhagavad Gītā* is called "*Advaita amṛta varṣiṇīm,*" the nectarous shower of Advaita. Advaita is the highest experience of seeing all forms in this universe as manifestations of the Supreme Being.

Amma abides in this state. Let us become Arjunas and drink this milk of *Gītā*. Drinking this glorious and ever-purifying milk, i.e. the teaching of *Gītā*, helps us attain the Supreme.

The *Bhagavad Gītā* is considered the fifth Vēda because it contains the essence of Vēdic teachings. It is considered especially sacred because it comes directly from Lord Kṛṣṇa. Just as Mother Gangā cascaded down from Lord Śiva's matted locks and purified the earth, so, too, Mother Gītā poured forth from Lord Kṛṣṇa's mouth to cleanse us of our sins, purify our minds, and take us back to our eternal home, *Ōm*.

Let us consider three important lessons from the *Bhagavad Gītā*:

1. Just before the commencement of the Mahābhārata War on the battlefield of Kurukṣētra, the Kaurava and Pāṇḍava armies stood facing each other. Arjuna told Lord Kṛṣṇa, "O Kṛṣṇa, please drive my chariot and place it in between the two armies. Let me see the warriors who have come to fight with us."

Although Kṛṣṇa was Arjuna's charioteer, He was the Lord Himself. Kṛṣṇa was the Commander; Arjuna and the others were just His instruments. But Arjuna had forgotten this. Instead, he tried to make the Lord his instrument.

In His infinite wisdom, Lord Kṛṣṇa placed His chariot where Arjuna could see his revered grand uncle, Bhīṣma, and his Guru, Drōṇa. The sight of these two people stirred strong feelings of attachment in Arjuna. Such is the power of *Māyā*, cosmic delusion. The idea of fighting with and possibly killing those whom he loved and venerated was so overwhelming that Arjuna became completely shattered.

We must ask ourselves: are we instruments in Amma's hands? Or are we using Her as an instrument to gain name and fame?

Later, Arjuna requested Lord Kṛṣṇa to accept him as His disciple, and surrendered totally to Him. Kṛṣṇa then dispelled his delusion by imparting the eternal teachings of the *Bhagavad Gītā*. Similarly, when we become Amma's instruments, we gradually become purified and attain both worldly prosperity and, finally, spiritual enlightenment.

2. Dhṛtarāṣṭra was a blind king. He symbolizes the mind, which is blind. Gāndhārī, his wife, symbolizes the intellect that becomes blind when wedded to the blind mind—that is the symbolic meaning of the blindfold she wears. When the desire-ridden mind (Dhṛtarāṣṭra) controls the intellect (Gāndhārī), hundreds of negative qualities and tendencies are produced. This is symbolized by the 100 sons, the Kauravas.

'*Dhṛta*' means firm; '*rāṣṭra*' means position. 'Dhṛtarāṣṭra' is thus one who holds firmly to position, like many political leaders. Let us not be like Dhṛtarāṣṭra, aggressively holding on to positions. Instead, let us hold on to Amma's feet, which alone give absolute peace and joy.

Conversely, the five Pāṇḍavas represent the positive qualities, which are generally outnumbered by the negative qualities and thoughts. They also represent the five senses. When these senses are guided by the Supreme, in the form of Lord Kṛṣṇa, victory is certain.

3. Arjuna's valiant son, Abhimanyu, was trapped in the *cakra-vyūham*, the circular military formation that the Kaurava army adopted. While Abhimanyu was in his mother Subhadra's womb, he had heard his father telling his mother about how to break and enter the cakravyūham. But before Arjuna could tell Subhadrā how to come out of it, Subhadrā had fallen asleep, and so, Arjuna had stopped. Thus, Abhimanyu never learned how to escape the cakravyūham. Trapped by the Kaurava army, he was killed.

The cakravyūham also has a symbolic meaning. It stands for the high circle, the circle of the rich and powerful. Having entered it, it is even more difficult to exit, and we become trapped. It is like trouble—easy to get into, but difficult to get out of! Creation is one big circle. Instead of forming or getting into small cliques—those stagnating and stinking small pools—let us, as children of the Divine Mother, identify ourselves more with the universal family.

Creation is an infinite circle. Countless galaxies circumambulate Lord Viṣṇu, forming a vast circle. Let us form one big circle around Amma, singing Her holy name and dancing in joy. As the galaxies finally merge into Lord Viṣṇu, may we all merge into Amma.

Retreating with Amma

Some time ago, a devotee told me that he was going to attend a *Bhagavad Gītā* retreat. Playing on the word 'retreat,' I quipped, "The *Bhagavad Gītā* never teaches us to retreat. She advises, encourages and inspires us to go forward!" Any day is good for beginning the study of the *Gītā* but the best day to start, I joked, was March 4th ("march forth").

Indeed, the *Bhagavad Gītā* teaches us never to retreat or run away from the Battle of Life, but gives us divine strength to move forward and face the challenges of life with a calm and peaceful mind.

The *Bhagavad Gītā* says,

> *yam labdhvā cāparam lābham*
> *manyatē nādhikam tataḥ*
> *yasmin sthitō na duḥkhēna*
> *guruṇāpi vicālyatē!*
>
> Obtaining it (infinite bliss), he feels there is nothing else to be gained. Established therein, he remains unshaken even in the most trying circumstances. (6.22)

We can discern this imperturbable quality in Amma. Many CEOs visit Her to unburden themselves and find relief from tension. Amma is probably the only CEO who never complains about tension or stress, and is thus a role model of an ideal leader. In this sense, She is like Goddess Pārvatī. 'Pārvatī' means one who resides on the *parvata* (mountain). The implied meaning is one who has the unshakeable or immoveable quality of a mountain, for a mountain is also called 'acala'—unshakeable or unmoving.

The *Bhagavad Gītā* compares the knower of Truth to an ocean that never overflows, even when all the rivers in the world flow into it. So, too, a Satguru is never perturbed by any number of problems; nothing can ever disturb Her quietude.

A story illustrates this quality of imperturbability. One morning, a Japanese spiritual master was conducting a class for his disciples and devotees in his āśram, which was located in an earthquake-prone area. Suddenly, there was a violent tremor. All the devotees ran outside, fearing the āśram building may collapse, but the Master remained still in his seat, calm and composed. When the tremor stopped, the devotees returned shamefacedly and asked the Master, "O Master, why didn't you run outside like us?"

The Master smiled and replied, "I *did* run! The only difference is all of you ran outside... I ran inside!"

The Master withdrew to a place deep within himself, beyond the body and mind. All great spiritual masters have perfected this technique of withdrawing themselves from the outside world and remaining established in their true nature—the *Ātma*, or Pure Consciousness. The *Bhagavad Gītā* illustrates this principle with a beautiful simile:

yadā samharatē cāyam
kūrmoŝngānīva sarvaśaḥ

> ... like the tortoise pulling in its limbs from all sides. (2.58)

This inner retreat is the best of all retreats, for the Self is an indestructible, impregnable fortress. Retreats offer physical and mental rest and rejuvenation, and purify the exhausted and dissipated mind.

Have you seen a fight between a cobra and a mongoose? It is most interesting. A cobra is long and powerful, and strikes with bullet speed. A mongoose is a small creature, but it can move and dodge fast. Every time the cobra strikes the mongoose, the mongoose darts into a nearby bush, nibbles on some herb, and returns, ready for the fight. The cobra finally gets tired and the mongoose overcomes it. We, children of Amma, are like the mongoose, and Her āśrams are like the nearby bush where, stung by the cobra of worldliness, the rare herbs of Amma's darśan, arcana, mantra japa, bhajans and meditation can heal us.

A retreat in Amma's divine presence is a rare treat. Firstly, the food (*prasād*) comes to us directly from Her divine hands. Secondly, the retreat is a re-treatment—in Her presence, we are once again ensconced in a calm and peaceful atmosphere. When we tune our mind into Amma's divine presence, the mind enjoys a rejuvenating bath. The mind is also fed with the most nutritious and tasty food in the form of Amma's talks and bhajans. Thirdly, in the presence of a Satguru like Amma, we can go deep into meditation, i.e. deep into ourselves.

Many of us have had joyful experiences of retreats. During Amma's South and North Indian Tours, those in the tour group stop for lunch and evening tea with Amma. These are brief retreats. Everyone crowds around Amma, who practices new bhajans, meditates with Her children, initiates a question-and-answer session, jokes, offers valuable advice on spiritual practices, and then distributes lunch or dinner prasād.

Our bodies enjoy a good rest in deep sleep, but the mind may not necessarily be rested. A person who goes to sleep with a disturbed mind wakes up gloomy and depressed. Modern psychiatrists can help to a limited extent. Only the Guru can flush out all the negativities of the mind.

Retreats and sādhana camps teach us more about ourselves. They also help us understand that true happiness lies within and in giving rather than receiving. Arcana, yōga, classes on the scriptures and Amma's teachings, Amma's bhajans—these are the real treats, food for the soul. Amma says, "Unless we give up the taste of the tongue, we can never experience the taste of the Self." In Her presence, giving up the taste of the tongue is easy. Surprisingly, what we find most difficult to renounce is the mobile phone! We carry it even into the prayer hall during Amma's satsangs and bhajans. Retreat means totally disconnecting or withdrawing from the outer world.

May we all understand the true meaning and purpose of retreats, and find time to participate in them. Retreats give us divine strength, peace and joy. May we also learn to share joy and peace with others in the world.

What It Means to be a Brāhmin

svasti prajābhyaḥ paripālayantām
nyāyyēna mārgēṇa mahīm mahīṣāḥ
gō brāhmaṇēbhyaḥ śubhamastu nityam
lōkāḥ samastāḥ sukhinō bhāvantu

May the subjects live in harmony.
May kings rule the earth with justice.
May cows and Brāhmins live auspiciously.
May all beings in all the worlds be happy.

The lines quoted above are the *śanti mantra*, or prayer chanted for universal peace. Quite regrettably, there have been instances of people misquoting or misinterpreting our scriptures with the sole intention of denigrating our religion. One trick often resorted to is singling out a line from a mantra to create a distorted picture. For example, the third line from the above-mentioned mantra is often quoted in isolation: "May the cows and Brāhmins live auspiciously." It sounds prejudiced, at the least; or like proof of scriptural sanction for social elitism, at the worst. The other lines, which offer a context for correctly understanding the mantra, are conveniently overlooked by the unscrupulous.

Moreover, there are compelling reasons why cows and Brāhmins have been singled out for special mention. In the olden days, cows were the wealth of society. They give an abundance of nutritious milk and demand relatively little by way of food or maintenance. From milk comes ghee, which is the most important offering in a yajña for it was considered the food of the gods. Ghee is also a key ingredient used in the preparation of Ayurvēdic medicine and *pañcagavyam*, a dairy product taken for purifying one's body. Even cow dung has numerous uses: as manure, medicine and paving for the floor, among other uses. For this reason, our scriptures place cows on par with mothers, who give the most to her children, expecting nothing in return.

Cows also produce bulls, which were necessary in ancient agrarian societies for plowing. In addition, bulls were the only means of transportation for the average person then. Cattle have even made their way into the pantheon of gods: Lord Śiva's vehicle is Nandi, the divine bull, while Śrī Kṛṣṇa is often pictured against a cow.

As for the Brāhmins of old, they were steeped in scriptural learning, and thus, imparted wisdom to people. They lived a spartan life, giving the maximum and taking the minimum.

The *Vajrasūci Upaniṣad* describes a Brāhmin as someone who has become one with Brahman, the Supreme. Such a person sets the best example of extreme selflessness and compassion, for he or she has had the direct experience that the entire universe is the cosmic form of God. The *Purāṇas* enumerate the lives of many such mahātmās like Vasiṣṭha, Atri, Viśvāmitra and Bharadvāja.

The scriptures do not say that being born into a Brāhmin family alone makes one a Brāhmin. In fact, they make it clear that it is one's virtues and deeds that determine if one is a Brāhmin. Sage Vyāsa, who codified and preserved Vēdic knowledge and thus enabled the transmission of Vēdic wisdom, was born to a fisherwoman, Satyavatī. The great sage Parāśara thought this virtuous girl fittest to be the mother of his would-be, great son.

Actually, one who is extremely pure-hearted and selfless, utilizing his or her knowledge to serve others, is a Brāhmin and, therefore, needs to be protected. In that sense, a scientist who labors selflessly, day and night, to discover a cure for cancer can be considered a Brāhmin. We can also become Brāhmins if we want, though perhaps not in the eyes of society, but in a finer sense. Many, in fact, do. For example, pilgrims who trek to see Lord Ayyappa on top of Mount Śabari observe a 41-day vow of celibacy, vegetarianism, physical and mental cleanliness, and prayers a few times a day. They are, in fact, following a Brāhminical lifestyle. There is no reason why they cannot continue to maintain such a lifestyle. We, too, can become Brāhmins by adopting such a life.

We may even assert that the Brāhmin *pūjāri* (priest) of old was not prejudiced against people of other castes. On the contrary, the priest worshipped at the shrine of purity, no matter who the object of adoration was. This is evident from the fact that the Brāhmin worshipped the 12 *Aḷvārs* (Vaiṣnava saints) and 63 *Nāyanmārs* (Śaiva saints) – who were from different castes, including outcastes. The statuettes of these saints decorate the outer walls of the *sanctum sanctorum*, which devotees circumambulate reverentially.

There is an interesting story, culled from the annals of Kēraḷa history, that demonstrates the greater importance given to virtues and deeds over the caste into which one was born. The story concerns the lives of the 12 children born to Varuci, a Brāhmin, and his wife, a tribal woman. All 12 children were brought up by different foster-parents belonging to the different castes. After the children grew up, they would meet once a year in the house of Agnihōtri, the eldest brother, who had been brought up by Brāhmin foster-parents. The occasion of the yearly meeting was the death anniversary of their departed parents. They would perform the rites together, eat dinner together and spend the night at Agnihōtri's house. His siblings would then depart the next morning.

On one such occasion, Agnihōtri's Brāhmin relatives expressed displeasure over his lower-caste brothers staying over. When they asked Agnihōtri to wake his sleeping brothers up and dismiss them from the house, he suggested that they take on the unpleasant task themselves. When the relatives went from room to room, they found Lord Viṣṇu Himself reclining where each of the brothers had been sleeping.

Every human being—in fact, all animate and inanimate things in the world—is a manifestation of divinity. Agnihōtri was a true Brāhmin, who beheld divinity in everything and who treated everyone as different forms of God.

Another incident, one closer to home, illustrates how a true Brāhmin is one who has realized Brahman. Years ago, when the āśram was financially poor and struggling to make ends meet, Amma would donate one house to a poor person every year on Her birthday. Once, the beneficiary of one such house stopped some brahmacārīs from crossing her courtyard; they were wheeling a handcart loaded with sand for construction work, and her courtyard offered a short cut to the construction site. When they angrily reported the matter to Amma, She just laughed and advised them to take the longer route. A few years later, when She learned that this woman was having financial problems, Amma gave her a job in our hospital. This is the nature of a Brāhmin. Amma, who sees only the pure Self shining in each being, had no dislike or aversion toward this lady. Amma is truly the best among *brahmaniṣṭas*, or those who know the Supreme.

Just as we venerate cows and Brāhmins for their spirit of "giving the maximum and taking the minimum," we worship Amma because She is an apotheosis of that creed. May the tribe of such great souls increase!

Let us pray to Amma to bless us, so that we may be more like Her—selfless and loving, considering the entire universe to be Her own family—and eventually merge in Her infinite being, the Brahman.

Expansiveness

"We live in a world that has narrowed into a neighborhood before it has broadened into a brotherhood!"

This insightful statement by Lyndon B. Johnson, the 36th President of the USA, is as relevant today as when he uttered it. People say that science and technology have brought countries and people closer. This is true only to a limited extent. Yes, we can easily contact or communicate with someone thousands of miles away. But can we accept everyone as our own? We have heard the word 'mahātmā,' but have rarely pondered over the meaning of the word. A mahātmā is one whose heart has expanded to accommodate all of creation. That is why mahātmās are rare.

People called Gāndhiji a mahātmā because he dedicated his life to Indians and the downtrodden. Amma's life is not only for Indians and people of other nationalities but for all living beings in this universe. In Amma's mystic song, *'Ānanda Vīthiyil,'* She sings, "Seeing nothing as apart from my own Self..." Her Self has become everything. Her compassion has no selfish intention. She sees all Her children as part of Her own cosmic form or body. The Divine Mother is called *"avyāja karuṇā mūrtī"* ("embodiment of pure compassion") (*Laḷitā Sahasranāma*, 992).

There was a mahātmā who lived in a forest. The king of the land, who was not very pious, met the mahātmā during a hunt. The king contemptuously asked him, "What's so great about you? I have a vast kingdom, power and riches. You have nothing!"

The mahātmā said, "Come, let's go for a walk. I will explain matters to you." The mahātmā and the king walked together for a long time until they reached the border of the kingdom. The mahātmā continued walking into the neighboring kingdom, but the king stopped and said, "I cannot step into that kingdom. If I am caught, I might even be executed!"

The mahātmā laughed and said, "That's the difference between you and me. Look over there: a grand reception is waiting for me!" With these words, the mahātmā walked away. The king realized the difference between the limited power of a 'ruler' and the infinite power of a God-realized saint.

There is a beautiful saying:

svagṛhē pūjyatē mūrkhaḥ
svagrāmē pūjyatē prabhuḥ
svadēśē pūjyatē rājā
vidvān sarvatra pūjyatē

An imbecile is celebrated in his own home.
A lord is respected in his own town.
A king is worshipped in his own country.
A learned man is honored everywhere!

In India, vehicles entering another state must pay tourist tax. Buses from Kēraḷa entering Karnāṭaka must pay around ₹500 per person. During Amma's Indian tours, more than 500 people, including āśram residents and devotees, accompany Her. We are thus liable to pay a tax of more than ₹2.5 *lakhs* (₹250,000). But because Amma is a state guest of the Karnāṭaka government, this tax is waived. Similarly, most of the other Indian states also do not collect this tourist tax from the āśram group. Hence, Amma's children enjoy a share of the honor the states bestow on Her.

Śrī Rāma and Śrī Kṛṣṇa were adored by their subjects, not because they were kings but because they were divine incarnations. Amma is worshipped not because She has many āśrams and institutions, but because of the power of Her Universal Motherhood. Her World Tours bring people together in a spirit of love and harmony.

Where there are two or more intelligent beings, there will usually be conflict. Even in *Indra-lōka*—the world of Indra, the king of the gods—there was conflict between Indra and Sūrya, the sun god. Their enmity extended to their sons. When Vali, Indra's son, clashed with Sugrīva, Sūrya's son, Vali died. But just before he passed away, the two renounced their enmity and reconciled because of Lord Rāma.

Despite their differences, the gods were always ready to give up their differences when Lord Viṣṇu or Lord Śiva intervened. Similarly, Amma's children strive to give up their differences for Amma's sake because of their intense devotion to Her. The capital of Lord Rāma's kingdom was Ayōdhyā, which literally means 'without conflict.' Let us remember that we are all members of a single spiritual community, ABC: Amma's Blessed Children. In this way, we too can recreate Ayōdhyā, wherever we may be.

Lord Kṛṣṇa's eternal teachings in the *Bhagavad Gītā* can be summed up in the words, "*mām anusmara yudhya ca*"—"Remember Me and fight" (8.7). The real enemy is within—the ego and its offspring, negative thoughts. A constant awareness that we are all Amma's children enables us to focus on our own weaknesses instead of finding fault with others. When we win this battle, our hearts will become Amṛtapuri—a shrine to Amma—and Ayōdhyā—a sanctuary of peace.

Beware (Be Aware of) Anger

Once, on Her way to the Brahmasthānam Festival at Mangalore, Amma stopped at the Kāñhangāḍ Amṛta Vidyālayam (school) for evening tea, meditation and bhajan practice. During the question-and-answer session, a devotee asked, "Is it wrong to get angry with Amma?"

The question revealed her purity of mind, child-like simplicity and straightforwardness. I was reminded of a beautiful poem:

> I was angry with my friend,
> I told my wrath, my wrath did end,
> I was angry with my foe:
> I told it not, my wrath did grow.
>
> —William Blake

The devotee then explained why she was angry. Because of a small communication gap between her and the devotees organizing the program, she could not get Amma's darśan! Usually, those who travel with Amma don't go for darśan because of the huge crowds that come to see Her. However, Amma had told the devotees accompanying Her that they could come if they really felt like having darśan, but that darśan would be brief because of the huge crowds.

For us—Amma's children—Amma is the living God. Remembering this, let us try to give Her the best. Śrī Rāmakṛṣṇa Paramahamsa once said, "Whatever you offer God comes back to you multiplied a thousand times. So be careful what you offer Him!"

Nevertheless, God's compassion is so great that, as our holy books say, 'Every emotion directed towards God with concentration and intensity gets purified.' The gōpīs of Vṛndāvan directed their intense love towards Lord Kṛṣṇa and attained liberation. Kamsa, who knew that he was to die at Kṛṣṇa's hands and continuously thought of Him with intense fear, was finally killed and became liberated. Śiśupāla, who developed intense hatred towards Lord Kṛṣṇa, fought against the Lord, was killed by the Lord, and thus became eternally free.

We are really blessed to be with Amma. In Her luminous presence, our negative tendencies become revealed to us, and we sincerely make efforts to remove them. Amma puts us in situations and circumstances that make us aware of our imperfections. Gradually, we become purified in Her divine presence. The beginning of our progress is becoming aware of our false values and the low tendencies within us.

Many years ago, during one of Amma's foreign tours, when I was Brahmacārī Satyātma Caitanya, dressed in the yellow robes of initiated brahmacārīs/brahmacāriṇīs, there were occasions when I became very angry. I felt sad and decided to ask Amma when She returned why She had given the yellow cloth to someone as short-tempered as me.

When Amma returned after the tour, I went for darśan with the intention of asking Her this question. When my turn came, She hugged me, put me on Her lap and announced, "I am going to give him *sanyāsa!*"

The beginning of progress is becoming aware, more and more aware. This is possible only in the presence of an enlightened master like Amma. In Her presence, we can slowly feel the change taking place within us, the cloud within us getting cleared by the winds of divine grace. Finally, we discover Her divine presence within us in the form of pure awareness, making us realize that She is present in all beings in the same form. This realization alone binds us all together as one family and thus helps us fill it with peace and joy.

"Amma, may all beings be kind to me!"

"Amma, may all beings be kind to me!"—this is the attitude we all have. We want everyone to be kind to us.

There is a Vēdic prayer that goes like this: "Let the wind be sweet to me. So, too, the oceans, the plants (which give me food), the cows..."

Amma says that we should be kind to everyone in this universe. We can be called human only if we develop the ability to see unity in diversity, all beings in this universe being interdependent, and share what we have with our fellow beings. *Paśyati iti paśuḥ*—That which just sees is the animal; *mananāt manuṣyaḥ*—that which not only sees, but also observes and learns from the world is a human being.

Recently, I read an amusing poem called 'Darwin's Mistake:'

Three Monkeys sat on a coconut tree,
And discussed matters which are said to be,
Said one to the other, "Brother, I hear a rumor
That Man descended from our noble race,
The very idea is a disgrace.
For no monkey ever beat his children, nor deserted his wife.
No monkey ever built fences around coconut trees,
Allowing the fruits to perish.
And if starvation forced a monkey to steal,
No monkey took another monkey's life.

No Wonder! Man certainly descended,
But not from us!"

Some have certainly *descended* from the human to the animal level! And that is when God also descends to the level of human beings in order to raise them from the animal level back to the level of humanity, and then gradually to the divine level, from which they will never fall again. This descent of the Divine is called 'Avatār' in Sanskrit.

"Be a God-like giver, not a dog-like receiver" – This is the wonderful message behind Amma's life. She is the most wonderful giver, one who has no thought of taking anything. Through Her life, Amma has showered us with divine grace. She has made Her āśram a pipeline connecting the haves with the have-nots.

Once, a king ordered all the lions and tigers to be killed because he thought they were cruel. The result was that the population of deer and other herbivorous animals grew, affecting the plant and vegetable kingdom. If we kill snakes, the population of rats will increase.

Everywhere in nature, we can see a perfect balance. It is human beings who create an imbalance in creation.

Avatārs come to restore the imbalance created by human beings in creation. Nature will bless us if we contribute to the balance in creation, by not taking more than we need. Amma alone can teach us this wonderful life-giving formula. Look at Her life. Others might be able to take away the wealth that is outside us, but not the wealth within us. The whole world kneels before one who has discovered the wealth within Herself.

When the Buddha used to walk the streets, begging from door to door, people who saw him used to say, "Look! He holds a begging bowl but walks like a king! What a great wonder!" When I read this many years ago, I wanted to meet such a person. When I had Amma's darśan the first time, I met just such a Guru. At that time, Her āśram was a tiny plot of land, covering less than one square kilometer!

Swāmi Vivēkānanda's experiences when he first arrived in the USA come to mind. He was sitting in the streets with his stomach and pockets empty, when the wealthy couple, Mr. and Mrs. George Hale, came out of their palatial home to the street, drawn to this serene monk from India. They invited him into their home, and from then on looked after him well and did everything for him. Swāmi Vivēkānanda did not undergo any personality development course. He was trained by a wonderful master, Śrī Rāmakṛṣṇa Paramahamsa. This is what a Satguru like Amma can do for us—bring out the divine nature lying dormant in us.

Happy New Ears

In many Indian languages, a person who talks too much is called a "knife," probably because he/she kills others with the tedium of his/her talk! The more garrulous among them is labeled a "sword" or even "a rusted sword!"

It is no accident that God has given us two ears and one mouth. It indicates that we should listen twice as much as we talk.

Tulsīdās says that human ears are to be used mainly for listening to God's name—the names and stories of Śrī Rāma—and other satsangs. Actually, it is not only Tulsīdās; every Guru and mahātmā say the same thing: that the best ears are those that delight in listening to the Lord's names and talk of the Lord.

Amma says, "The best ears are not those that wear beautiful earrings but those that listen to the sufferings of others."

Swāmi Amṛtaswarupānanda once said in a talk, "Look at how Amma listens to the words of even a small child. She pays so much attention to him!"

If singing and speaking are an art and talent, so, too, is listening! We might think listening is easy, but we are mistaken. Listening to others is very difficult. Generally, people want to talk when others are talking to them. We unconsciously interrupt, not realizing how rude, impolite and discourteous we are.

I read about an experiment conducted by some well-known psychologists. Two prominent speakers were made to engage in a dialogue, which was recorded. An analysis of the discussion revealed that what seemed like a dialogue was actually two monologues; there was little connection between what one said and how the other responded. When one person spoke, the other would mechanically say, "Yes, of course!" or "Ah, very true!" However, the second person was not actually listening but busy thinking about what he would say when the other person stopped.

In the *Bhagavad Gītā*, Lord Kṛṣṇa listens to a distressed Arjuna in order to bring relief and healing to the latter. The divine psychologist allows His human patient to vent all his sorrows and confusions, and thus unburden himself. Arjuna thus gives a long 'discourse' in chapter 1 (from verses 29 – 47, i.e. 18 verses) and chapter 2 (verses 4 – 8, i.e. five verses) to all-knowing Kṛṣṇa, who listens with infinite patience. He then imparts to Arjuna the eternal teachings, clearing Arjuna's confusion, lifting his despondency, and infusing him with infinite spiritual strength.

Most of us have seen Amma patiently listening not only to the sufferings of millions of people who come to Her, but also to some educated 'Arjunas' giving lengthy 'sermons' to Amma, forgetting Her all-knowing nature! Amma does not only tell us about the "best ears," She also practices what She preaches!

One of the āśram bhajans contains the following line:

> *kuñjurumbin kālsvanavum śraviccīḍum kṛpārāśē...*
>
> O compassionate Mother, who can hear the footsteps of even an ant...

Gaṇapati has *cāmara karṇa*, the fan-like ears of an elephant. They symbolize His capacity to listen to any amount of sufferings of His devotees, even those in distant places.

How much time we have wasted listening to meaningless talk! Study of the scriptures is a sacred duty, both to Amma and to ourselves. Amma is not only our Mother but our Guru as well. She is waiting patiently for us to evolve so that we become eligible for *mōkṣa* (spiritual liberation). The scriptures say, "Having purified the mind through selfless actions and worship, one should approach one's Guru with humility and total surrender. One should sit at the feet of the Guru and receive *ātma upadēśa*, advice and guidance on how to know one's true nature. The way to this knowledge lies through *śravaṇam* (listening), *mananam* (reflection) and *nididdhyāsanam* (contemplation)." Let us pledge to use our ears mainly to listen to the scriptures (Amma's advice), the glories of the Lord, and devotional music.

Bhakti Yōga, the Path of Devotion, comprises nine types of devotion known as *nava-vidha-bhakti*:

> *śravaṇam kīrtanam viṣṇōh*
> *smaraṇam pādasēvanam*
> *arcanam vandanam dāsyam*
> *sakhyam ātmanivēdanam*

> Listening (to the stories of Viṣṇu), singing or chanting His holy name,
> Thinking of Him, serving His sacred feet,
> Worshipping Him with flowers, prostrating to Him, developing an attitude of servitude,
> Looking upon Him as one's constant companion, and surrendering oneself completely to Him.

Note that bhakti begins with *śravaṇam*, listening to the glories and the divine names of the Lord.

The *bhakti śāstras* (devotional scriptures) say that God enters our hearts through our ears, i.e. when we listen to the stories of the Lord. When Sage Śukadēv was about to start narrating the *Bhāgavatam*, many great ṛṣis and even gods came to listen to the narration. Let us also develop the habit of listening to the scriptures and chanting the Lord's names. Nothing else can give us greater joy.

Tulsīdās says that the ears of one who does not listen to the glories of the Lord are only holes where snakes reside! In other words, anything else that enters the ears is poisonous. He further says, the mouth that does not chant the holy name of God is as good as a frog's mouth, which opens only to swallow insects! In other words, the mouth is not just for eating. Eyes that refuse to see the enchanting form of the Lord are only like the 'eyes' on peacock feathers, i.e. unseeing. If Tulsīdās saw us with our ears constantly covered by mobile phones, what would he have thought of us?

In Amṛtapuri, God enters not only through the ears but eyes also. The ears are feasted every Monday, Tuesday and Friday, when Amma conducts a question-and-answer session. In other places that She visits, She gives spiritual discourses, which are food for the soul. In all places, our eyes can meditate on Her physical form. One whose mind is constantly focused on Amma and has absorbed Her completely does not need to study the scriptures, but this is very difficult. Most people need to study the scriptures in order to know Amma and ourselves better.

A question may arise in the minds of devotees, "When Amma Herself gives spiritual discourses, is there any need for Her disciples and devotees to give talks also?"

The answer is, there are certain things that Amma will not say; we, Her children, have to say them to devotees. For example, Amma's satsang often begins with the words "*Makkaḷ ellām iviḍe etti*"—"My children have all reached here." But we can say, "*Ammayuḍe makkaḷ ettēṇḍa iḍattil etti*"—"Amma's children have reached the true destination," i.e. Amma's divine presence. For us, who else other than Amma can take us to our eternal abode? In order to understand that one can realize one's true nature as the immortal self only through the Guru's grace and not through self-effort alone, one needs to learn the scriptures from a qualified teacher. Thus, śravaṇam is necessary.

Let us pray to Amma to give us also the capacity and patience to listen to others' sufferings and bring them to Amma. When we hear their sufferings, we can offer them one common solution: "Please come to Amma and get Her darśan. She will remove all your sufferings and give you infinite peace, joy and bliss."

Postface

Amṛta Sūtram

Amma's āśram in Bangalore is a beautiful and tranquil place for meditation. Early every morning and late at night, I sit in the corridor outside my room, facing a jackfruit tree in the āśram's courtyard. I remember what Amma said, "Bhakti is like a jackfruit tree; the fruits grow on the trunk of the tree, low enough for our hands to reach. You don't have to climb on top to pluck the fruits."

Amṛta Sūtra![44] The Guru's teachings are usually given in a few words. The disciple must reflect on them and introspect in order to understand the teachings.

Reflecting on Amma's teaching on the jackfruit tree, I learned many things...

One can experience the fruits of devotion—*viz.* joy and peace—early on in the spiritual journey to mōkṣa, whereas in the path of jñāna, one can experience joy and peace only at the end of the spiritual journey.

The jackfruit tree is sacred. Its wood is used in *hōmas*, sacrificial fires. Trees also give without receiving; they live only for others. In his *Rāmcaritmanas*, Tulsīdās says,

santa viṭāpa saritā giri dharaṇī
parahita hētu sabanha kai karaṇī

44 A sūtra is an epigram containing spiritual wisdom.

> Saints, trees, rivers, mountains and the earth exist only and always for the benefit of others. (7.125.3)

Spiritual masters teach that the whole of creation is a manifestation of the Supreme Being.

> *puruṣa ēva idam sarvam*
> *yad bhūtam yac ca bhavyam*
>
> All these are manifestations of that Supreme Puruṣa, all that was in the past and all that will be in the future! (*Śrī Puruṣa Sūktam*, 2)

Mother Nature silently teaches us the great quality of sharing with others. We owe Her an immensely great debt of gratitude. As Swāmi Vivēkānanda memorably said, "They alone live who live for others. Others are more dead than alive!"

In the olden days, when brahmacārīs graduated from their Gurukulas at about the age of 24, they were already aware of their duties to the world: "We have taken so much from the world. We have a duty to give back what little we can." They knew the ṛṣis had given them knowledge, that the gods, their parents and their ancestors sustained their life, that other human beings and even the flora and fauna have all contributed to their growth. Thus, keenly aware that they owed a lot to the world, they performed *pañca yajñas.*[45] Thus they became part of the cycle of give and take intrinsic to the universal family.

---

45 Five sacred duties performed to live in harmony with the world. They are dēva yajña (duty to God), pitṛ yajña (duty to the family and ancestors), brahma

Recently, when I was in Eṭṭimaḍai, Coimbatore, I met Jay Mishra, a devotee who manages some of our āśram projects. I asked him, "Are you here to conduct classes?"

He said, "No! I am waiting for Swāmi Rāmakṛṣṇānandaji, who is going to the Philippines to hand over a check for a million dollars to the cyclone victims' relief fund!" He continued, "I'm also here to meet someone who is an expert in water purification. Amma told us that one of our main projects should be water purification, because in future, there might be a scarcity of drinking water!"

Without water, we cannot survive. The ancient spiritual masters recognized this, and that was why they worshipped water along with other natural elements, seeing them all as manifestations of divinity:

> *ōm śam nō mitraḥ śam varuṇaḥ*
> *śam nō bhavatu aryamā*
> *śam na indrō bṛhaspatiḥ…*
> *namaste vāyō…*

> Ōm. May Mitra (Sun god) be propitious to us. May Varuṇa (Rain god) be propitious to us.
> May the honorable Aryama (ancestors) be propitious to us.
> May Indra (leader of the gods) and Bṛhaspati (Guru of the gods) be propitious to us.
> Salutations to Vāyu (Wind god).

---

yajña (duty to the Vēdic culture); manuṣya yajña (duty to fellow human beings) and bhūta yajña (duty to the ecosystem).

There was a sage named Vāmadēva who spoke little. He led a quiet life sowing seeds and planting saplings. Even when he was 108 years old, he continued to plant and sow. Amused, people asked him, "Revered sir, you are 108 years old. You won't live to eat the apples from the trees that grow out of the seeds you sow. Why do you waste time?"

Sage Vāmadēva smiled and said, "I have eaten the fruits from trees that others planted in the past; so have all of you. The seeds that I sow will become fruit-bearing trees for the future generation!"

The listeners, realizing the wisdom and generosity of the sage, fell at the ṛṣi's feet. When Sage Vāmadēva was about to leave his body, his devotees begged him to teach them something. The compassionate ṛṣi bequeathed 20 mantras, which later came to be known as *Īśāvāsya Upaniṣad*, one of the most important Upaniṣads. The first mantra is most famous:

> *īśāvāsyam idam sarvam,*
> *yat kiñca jagatyām jagat*
>
> This whole universe is pervaded by the Supreme Being.

We might not have attained the vision of all-pervading divinity yet. Nevertheless, hearkening to the wisdom of the spiritual masters, let us revere Mother Nature and do our duty by Her.

Gazing at the evergreen jackfruit, I felt more deeply than ever before that Amma has given me much, not least by way of Her immortal teachings. One can never repay the debt to the Guru. Be that as it may, I have tried to share some of the wisdom I have gleaned from Her through the pages of this book. I pray that with Her grace, these humble words inspire devotion to God in your hearts.

Glossary

ācārya Religious teacher.

adharma Unrighteousness. Deviation from natural harmony.

Ādi Śankarācārya Saint who is believed to have lived between the eighth and ninth centuries CE, and who is revered as a Guru and chief proponent of the ***Advaita*** (non-dual) philosophy.

Ādiparāśaktī Primal, supreme power, personified as the Divine Mother.

Advaita Not two; non-dual; philosophy that holds that the *jīva* (individual soul) and *jagat* (universe) are ultimately one with *Brahman*, the Supreme Reality.

Agni Fire God and deity of speech.

Akbar Emperor of the Mughal dynasty in India who ruled from 1556 – 1605 CE.

Amala Bhāratam A 'Clean India' Campaign that Amma launched on Her 57th Birthday (September 27th, 2010).

Amma Malayāḷam word for 'mother.'

amṛta Nectar of immortality.

Amṛtapuri International headquarters of the Mātā Amṛtānandamayī Maṭh, located at Amma's birth place in Parayakkaḍavu, Kollam, Kēraḷa, India.

Amṛtēśvarī Goddess of Immortality.

ārati Clockwise movement of a lamp aflame with burning camphor, to propitiate a deity, usually signifying the closing of a ceremonial worship.

arcana Chantin g of a litany of divine names.

Arjuna Third of the Pāṇḍava brothers and close companion of Kṛṣṇa.

āsana A seat, often a cloth on which a seeker meditates or does other spiritual practice; in *haṭha yōga*, a specific posture.

asat Unreality, not in the sense of that which does not exist, but that which does not have a permanent and abiding reality; changing forms.

āśram Monastery. Amma defines it as a compound: '*ā*'—'that' and '*śramam*'—'effort' (toward Self-realization); also one of the four stages of traditional life, viz. *brahmacārya* (celibate student life), *gārhasthya* (householder life), *vānaprastha* (secluded forest life) and *sanyāsa* (monastic life of renunciation).

Aṣṭavakra An ancient sage who was supposed to have been born with eight (*aṣṭa*) deformities (*vakra*) in his body. He was Guru of both King Janaka and Sage Yājñavalkya.

Aṣṭōttaram Litany of 108 attributes.

ātmā Self or Soul.

aum/ōm Primordial sound in the universe; the seed of creation; the cosmic sound, which can be heard in deep meditation; the sacred mantra, taught in the Upaniṣads, which signifies Brahman, the divine ground of existence; in the Mā-Ōm meditation that Amma teaches, the sound that one mentally synchronizes with every exhalation during the initial stages of meditation (before the sound dissolves into the breath).

avadhūta An enlightened person whose behavior transcends social norms.

avatār Divine incarnation.

avidyā Ignorance.

Ayōdhyā Ancient Indian city, birthplace of Rāma, and setting of part of the *Rāmāyaṇa.*

Ayyappa Hindu deity, born of the union of Śiva and Mōhinī, a female incarnation of Viṣṇu.

Bhagavad Gītā Literally, 'Song of the Lord,' it consists of 18 chapters of verses in which Lord Kṛṣṇa advises Arjuna. The advice is given on the battlefield of Kurukṣētra, just before the righteous Pāṇḍavas fight the unrighteous Kauravas. It is a practical guide to overcoming crises in one's personal or social life, and is the essence of Vēdic wisdom.

Bhaja Gōvindam Literally, 'Seek Gōvinda,' a popular eighth-century devotional composition by Ādi Śankarācārya.

bhajan Devotional song or hymn in praise of God.

bhakta Devotee.

bhakti Devotion for God.

Bhāratapuzha Second longest river in Kēraḷa.

bhāva Divine mood; attitude.

bhāvanā Imagination; 'calling into existence.'

Bhīṣma Character from the *Mahābhārata*; son of King Śantanu, and granduncle of both the Pāṇḍavas and Kauravas. During the Mahābhārata War, he fought on the side of the Kauravas.

bhukti Worldly prosperity.

Bīrbal Adviser in Akbar's court, he was well-known for his wit and wisdom.

Bōdhaka Guru Guru who initiates the disciple into a *mantra*.

Brahmā Lord of Creation in the Hindu Trinity.

Brahma-lōka The world of Brahmā, the Creator.

Brahmacārī Celibate male disciple who practices spiritual disciplines under a Guru. (Brahmacāriṇi is the female equivalent.)

Brahman Ultimate Truth beyond any attributes; the Supreme Reality underlying all life; the divine ground of existence.

Brahmasthānam Literally, 'place of Brahman.' The name of the temples Amma has consecrated in various parts of India and in Mauritius. The temple shrine features a unique four-faced idol that symbolizes the unity behind the diversity of divine forms.

Brāhmin Priest; a member of the first of the four hereditary castes. It is his duty to recite the Vēdas, to perform rituals and to teach the rest of the people by word and deed the true nature of dharma.

Buddha 'Awakened One;' from 'budh' (to know, to wake up); a reference to Sage Gautama Buddha.

Cāngdēv Saint with mystic powers who lived in the village of Vatēśvar in Mahārāṣtra, India.

caitanya Divine consciousness.

cakravyūham A multi-tier, circular defensive formation mentioned in the *Mahābhārata.*

cintanam Reflection.

Dakṣinamūrti Literally, 'South-facing One.' A manifestation of Lord Śiva as supreme awareness, understanding and knowledge, and as the teacher of yoga, music, wisdom and scriptural knowledge. Regarded as the first Guru.

Dakṣinēśvar Location of the Dakṣinēśvar Kāḷī Temple, near Kōlkaṭa, West Bengal. The temple is famous for its association with Śrī Ramakṛṣṇa Paramahamsa.

darśan Audience with a holy person or a vision of the Divine.

Daśaratha Father of Rāma.

dēva Deity.

Dēvakī Mother of Kṛṣṇa.

Dēvī Goddess/Divine Mother.

Dēvī Bhāva 'The Divine Mood of Dēvī,' the state in which Amma reveals Her oneness and identity with the Divine Mother.

dharma Literally, 'that which upholds (creation).' Generally used to refer to the harmony of the universe, a righteous code of conduct, sacred duty or eternal law.

dhyāna Meditation.

dīpasthambham Towering structure located in front of Hindu temples for lighting oil-lamps.

dōśa Indian pancake.

Drōṇa Also known as Drōṇācārya, he was the teacher of both the Pāṇḍavas and the Kauravas; a master of military arts.

Duryōdhana Eldest of the 100 sons of King Dhṛtarāṣṭra and Queen Gāndhārī; leader of the Kaurava clan; and claimant to the throne of Hastinapura.

Durgā Principal form of the Mother Goddess in Hinduism.

Dvāraka Capital of kingdom that Kṛṣṇa established after He left Mathura.

Ēknāth 16th-century saint, scholar and poet from Mahārāṣṭra, India.

Embracing the World Global network of regional humanitarian organizations inspired by the India-based humanitarian initiatives of the Mata Amritanandamayi Math.

Garuḍa Brahminy kite; mount (*vāhana*) of Lord Viṣṇu.

Gāndhārī Wife of Dhṛtarāṣṭra and mother of the Kauravas.

Gangā The Ganges River, considered sacred by the Hindus.

Gaṇēśa Popular deity in the Hindu pantheon and revered as remover of obstacles, patron of arts and sciences, and the deity of intellect and wisdom. Also known as Gaṇapati and Vināyaka.

Gāyatrī Vēdic mantra that invokes Sāvitrī, a solar deity.

Gōkul Village near Mathura where Kṛṣṇa spent His childhood.

gōpa Cowherd boy from Vṛndāvan.

gōpī Milkmaid from Vṛndāvan. The gōpīs were known for their ardent devotion to Lord Kṛṣṇa. Their devotion exemplifies the most intense love for God.

guṇa One of three types of qualities viz. ***satva***, ***rajas*** and ***tamas***. Human beings express a combination of these qualities. Satvic qualities are associated with calmness and wisdom, rajas with activity and restlessness, and tamas with dullness or apathy.

Guru Spiritual teacher.

Guru Gītā Hymn (in traditional Sānskṛt verse forms) that is a dialog between Lord Śiva, the primordial Guru, and Goddess Pārvatī, His consort and disciple. In this dialog, Lord Śiva expounds on the nature of the Guru, the power of the His grace, the importance of devotion and service to the Guru, and the ways in which the Guru leads the disciple to knowledge of the Self.

Gurukula Literally, the clan (kula) of the preceptor (Guru); traditional school where students would stay with the Guru for the entire duration of their studies (a period of about 12 years), during which the Guru would impart scriptural and academic knowledge as well as spiritual values.

Hanumān One of the foremost devotees of Rāma. He led an army of *vānaras* (monkeys) into Lanka, and helped to topple Rāvaṇa's regime.

harmonium Handheld Indian keyboard instrument.

haṭha yōga "Forceful yōga." Haṭha yōga is a system of physical, breathing and mental exercises meant for preparing the body and mind for meditation.

hōma Ritual wherein an oblation or religious offering is made into a sacrificial fire.

īśvara-kṛpā Divine grace.

Indra Leader of the ***dēvas***, and God of rain and thunderstorms.

iṣṭa-dēvatā Preferred form of divinity.

Jagadambā Mother of the Universe.

Janaka Father of Sītā and ruler of Mithila.

japa Repeated chanting of a mantra; also called *mantra japa.*

-ji Suffix denoting respect.

jīva / jīvātmā Individual Self or Soul.

jñāna Knowledge of the Truth.

jñāna yōga Path of knowledge, in which the knowledge of the identity between Brahman and the Self dawns on the basis of hearing (*śravaṇa*), reflection (*manana*) and meditation (*nididhyāsana*); this path is also known as *jñāna mārga.*

Jñānēśvar 13th-century saint, poet, philosopher and yōgī from Maharāṣṭra, India.

jñānī Knower of the Truth.

Kailāś "Abode of bliss." The four-faced Himālayan peak in Western Tibet; the earthly abode of Lord Śiva.

Kāka Bhuśuṇḍi A sagely crow regarded as the first narrator of the *Rāmāyaṇa.*

kaḷari Generally, a center for martial arts training; the temple where Amma used to hold Kṛṣṇa Bhāva and Dēvī Bhāva darśans; also, a temple enshrining a family deity.

Kāḷī Goddess of fearsome aspect; depicted as dark, wearing a garland of skulls, and a girdle of human hands; feminine of Kāla (time).

Kali Yuga see ***yuga***.

kalpa One day of Lord Brahmā; about 4.32 billion years; each kalpa is made up of 1,000 *mahāyugas*, and each *mahāyuga* is made up of four yugas. It spans the period from creation to dissolution; see ***yuga***.

Kamsa Maternal uncle of Kṛṣṇa who overthrew his father and usurped the throne of Mathura.

karma Action; mental, verbal or physical activity.

karma yōga The way of dedicated action, the path of selfless service; also known as *karma mārga.*

kīrtī Divine glory.

kṛpā Grace.

Kṛṣṇa From '*kṛṣ*,' meaning 'to draw to oneself' or 'to remove sin;' principal incarnation of Lord Viṣṇu. He was born into a royal family but raised by foster parents, and lived as a cowherd boy in Vṛndāvan, where He was loved and worshipped by His devoted companions, the gōpīs and gōpas. Kṛṣṇa later established the city of Dwāraka. He was a friend and advisor to His cousins, the Pāṇḍavas, especially Arjuna, whom He served as charioteer during the Mahābhārata War, and to whom He revealed His teachings as the *Bhagavad Gītā.*

Kubēra God of Wealth.

kumkum Saffron powder; used as a religious mark (on the forehead) by the devout.

Kurukṣētra Battlefield where the war between the Pāṇḍavas and Kauravas was fought; also, a metaphor for the conflict between good and evil.

Lakṣmaṇa Younger brother of Rāma.

Lakṣmī Goddess of wealth and prosperity, and consort of Viṣṇu.

līlā Divine play.

Mā 'Mother;' in the Mā-Ōm meditation that Amma teaches, 'Mā' is the sound that one mentally synchronizes with every inhalation during the initial stages of meditation (before the sound dissolves into the breath).

Mahābali A great ruler of demons, who attained God-realization through *ātmanivēdanam* (self-surrender).

Mahābhārata Ancient Indian epic that Sage Vyāsa composed, depicting the war between the righteous Pāṇḍavas and the unrighteous Kauravas.

maharṣi 'Great (*mahā*) ṛṣi.' See ***ṛṣi.***

mahātmā Literally, 'great soul.' Used to describe one who has attained spiritual realization.

Malayāḷam Language spoken in the Indian state of Kēraḷa.

mānasa pūja Ceremonial worship performed by visualization.

mantra A sound, syllable, word or words of spiritual content. According to Vēdic commentators, mantras were revealed to ***ṛṣis*** while they were in deep meditation.

Māyā Cosmic delusion, personified as a temptress. Illusion; appearance, as contrasted with Reality; the creative power of the Lord.

Mīrābāī 16th-century Hindu mystic and devotee of Lord Kṛṣṇa.

mōn 'Son' in Malayāḷam

mūrti (Divine) form.

Muruga Son of Lord Śiva, Hindu God of War, and commander-in-chief of the army of ***dēvas***. Also known as Subrahmaṇya, Kārtikēya and Skanda.

mukti Spiritual liberation

Nahuṣa King of the Aila dynasty who acquired sovereignty of the three worlds through sacrifices, austerities, scriptural study, self-restraint, and valor. Later, owing to arrogance, he was cursed to be reborn as a snake.

Nāmadēv Poet saint (1270 – 1350 CE) from Mahārāṣtra, India.

nava-vidha-bhakti Nine modes of devotion, *viz. śravaṇam* (hearing the Lord's glory), *kīrtanam* (chanting the Lord's name), *smaraṇam* (remembering the Lord and His divine play), *pādasēvanam* (serving the Lord's feet), *arcanam* (worshipping the Lord), *vandanam* (prostrating to the Lord), *dāsyam* (becoming a servant of the Lord), *sakhyam* (becoming a friend of the Lord) and *ātmanivēdanam* (surrendering wholly to the Lord).

ōm see ***aum***.

Pāṇḍavas Five sons of King Pāṇḍu, and cousins of Kṛṣṇa.

Paramahamsa 'Supreme Swan;' an epithet given to highly elevated saints owing to their power of discernment, i.e.

ability to see the Self in all forms. Paramahamsinī is the feminine equivalent.

Paramātmā Supreme Self.

Parāśaktī Supreme Power.

Parīkṣit Grandson of Arjuna. Owing to a rash act, he was cursed to die of snakebite. He spent the last week of his life listening to Śuka's enlightening spiritual discourses.

prārabdha The consequences of actions from previous lives that one is destined to experience in the present life.

prasād Blessed offering or gift from a holy person or temple, often in the form of food.

prēyas The pleasant, which detracts from one's spiritual well-being; often contrasted with ***śrēyas***.

pūja Ritualistic or ceremonial worship.

purāṇa puruṣa Ancient being, yet ever fresh and new.

Purāṇas Hindu folk narratives containing ethical and cosmological teachings relating to the gods, human beings and the world. The teachings revolve around five subjects: primary creation, secondary creation, genealogy, cycles of time and history. There are 18 major Purāṇas which are designated as Śaivite (centered on Lord Śiva), Vaiṣṇavite (centered on Lord Śiva) or Śakta (centered on Dēvī).

Pūrṇa Full or Whole / Spiritual fullness.

pūrṇakumbha Vessel filled with water, usually offered to welcome the Guru; used in rituals and also while receiving holy personages.

Puruṣa 'Man' in Malayāḷam; 'Supreme Self' in Sānskṛt.

rākṣas Demon.

Rāma The divine hero of the epic *Rāmāyaṇa*. An incarnation of Lord Viṣṇu, he is considered the ideal man of *dharma* and virtue. '*Ram*' means 'to revel;' one who revels in himself; the principle of joy within; also one who gladdens the hearts of others.

Ramaṇa Maharṣi Enlightened spiritual master (1879 – 1950) who lived in Tiruvaṇṇāmalai in Tamiḷ Nāḍu. He recommended Self-inquiry as the path to Liberation, though He approved of a variety of paths and spiritual practices.

Rāmāyaṇa A 24,000-verse epic poem on the life and times of Rāma.

rāsa līlā 'Dance of divine love,' wherein Lord Kṛṣṇa danced with Radha and each of the other ***gōpīs***.

Rāvaṇa King of Lanka, and primary antagonist in the *Rāmāyaṇa*.

ṛṣi Seer to whom mantras were revealed in deep meditation.

rūpam Form

Śabarimala Temple in Kēraḷa's Western Ghats dedicated to Lord Ayyappa.

sādhana Regime of disciplined and dedicated spiritual practice that leads to the supreme goal of Self-realization.

sādhak Spiritual aspirant or seeker.

Sahasranāma Sacred litany of thousand names.

Śakti Power; personification of the Universal Mother; principle of pure energy associated with Śiva, the principle of pure consciousness.

samādhi Literally, 'cessation of all mental movements;' oneness with God; a transcendental state in which one loses all sense of individual identity; union with Absolute Reality; a state of intense concentration in which consciousness is completely unified.

Śamīka Sage who was immersed in deep meditation when King Parīkṣit put a dead snake around the sage's neck for not responding to his call for water. The sage's son cursed Parīkṣit for his insolence.

samsāra Cycle of births and deaths; the world of flux; the wheel of birth, decay, death and rebirth.

samskāra The totality of one's personality traits that one has acquired as a result of conditioning over many lifetimes. This can also be taken to mean one's level of inner refinement or character; also milestone rituals.

Sanātana Dharma Literally, 'Eternal Religion' or 'The Eternal Way of Life,' the original and traditional name for Hinduism.

sangha Spiritual community.

sankalpa Divine resolve, usually used in association with mahātmās.

śānti Spiritual peace.

sanyāsa A formal vow of renunciation.

sanyāsī A monk who has taken formal vows of renunciation (sanyāsa); traditionally wears an ocher-colored robe, representing the burning away of all desires. The female equivalent is *sanyāsinī.*

śāstra Science; in the context of this book, authoritative scriptural texts.

Sat Eternal changeless principle.

Satguru Literally, 'true master.' One who, while still experiencing the bliss of the Self, chooses to come down to the level of ordinary people in order to help them grow spiritually.

satsang Being in communion with the Supreme Truth. Also being in the company of *mahātmās*, studying scriptures, listening to a spiritual talk or discussion, and participating in spiritual practices in a group setting.

satva See **guṇa**.

sēva Selfless service, the results of which are dedicated to God.

siddha Ascetic who has attained spiritual enlightenment.

siddhi Occult or miraculous power

Sītā Rāma's holy consort. In India, She is considered the ideal of womanhood.

Śiva Worshipped as the first and the foremost in the lineage of Gurus, and as the formless substratum of the universe in relationship to Śakti. He is the Lord of destruction in the Trinity of Brahmā (Lord of Creation), Viṣṇu (Lord of Sustenance), and Mahēśvara (Śiva).

śraddhā Attentiveness; faith.

śravaṇam Hearing the Lord's glory (see ***nava-vidha-bhakti)***; different from śravaṇa in ***jñāna yōga***.

śrēyas The good, which conduces to the spiritual well-being of a person; often contrasted with ***prēyas***.

Śrī A title of respect originally meaning 'divine,' 'holy' or 'auspicious;' now in modern India, simply a respectful form of address, similar to 'Mr.'

Śrī Laḷitā Sahasranāma Sacred litany of 1,000 names of Śrī Laḷitā Dēvī, the Supreme Goddess.

Śrīmad Bhāgavatam Also known as *Bhāgavatam* or *Bhāgavata Purāṇa* (meaning 'Sacred Tales of the Supreme Lord'), one of the Purāṇic texts of Hinduism. Contains stories of the incarnations of Viṣṇu, including the life and pastimes of Kṛṣṇa.

Śrī Rāmakṛṣṇa Paramahamsa A 19th century spiritual master from West Bengal, hailed as the apostle of religious harmony. He generated a spiritual renaissance that continues to touch the lives of millions.

sudarśana cakra A spinning, disk-like weapon; associated with Lord Viṣṇu.

Sudhāmaṇī Literally, 'gem of immortality;' the name that Amma's parents gave Her.

Śukadēv Son of Vyāsa and main narrator of the ***Bhāgavatam***.

sūtra An epigram containing spiritual wisdom.

svarūpam Essential nature.

swāmi Title of one who has taken the vow of ***sanyāsa***.

Swāmi Vivēkānanda

Chief monastic disciple of Śrī Rāmakṛṣṇa Paramahamsa.

Śyāmsundar Literally, 'dark and beautiful;' a name of Lord Kṛṣṇa.

tabla Pair of hand drums played in Indian music.

tapas Austerity, penance.

tēnga Coconut, which is often a token offering at shrines in Hindus temples.

tēngal Yearning.

tīrtham Sacred water body, often associated with a temple or deity.

triguṇas see ***guṇa***.

Tulsīdās 16th-century poet, saint and philosopher, well-known for the *Rāmcaritmanas*, a retelling of the Sānskṛt *Rāmāyaṇa*.

upadēśa Spiritual advice.

Upaniṣad The portions of the Vēdas dealing with Self-knowledge.

vāhana Vehicle or mount; often associated with a deity.

Vaḷḷikkāvu Village across the backwaters on the eastern side of the peninsula where the Amṛtapuri Āśram is located. Amma is sometimes referred to as 'Vaḷḷikkāvu Amma.'

Vāmana Small Brāhmin boy and incarnation of Lord Viṣṇu. He humbles King Mahābali when the latter conducts a ritual sacrifice. Vāmana asks for three paces of land. In two strides, Vāmana covers the earth and sky, and the netherworlds. He places His third step on Mahābali's head and pushes the king into the netherworlds.

vānara Monkey; in the *Rāmāyaṇa*, the *vānara sēna* (monkey brigade), headed by Hanumān, helps Lord Rāma in His mission of rescuing Sītā.

vāsanā Latent tendency or subtle desire that manifests as thought, motive and action; subconscious impression gained from experience.

Vasiṣṭha Great sage and Guru of Rāma.

Vasudēva Father of Kṛṣṇa.

Vāyu Wind God and presiding deity of touch.

Vēdānta 'The end of the Vēdas.' It refers to the Upaniṣads, which deal with the subject of Brahman, the Supreme Truth, and the path to realize that Truth.

Vēdas Most ancient of all scriptures, originating from God, the Vēdas were not composed by any human author but were 'revealed' in deep meditation to the ancient ṛṣis. These sagely revelations came to be known as Vēdas, of which there are four: Ṛg, Yajus, Sāma and Atharva.

Vēdic Of or pertaining to the ancient Vēdas.

vidyā Knowledge.

Viṣṇu Lord of Sustenance in the Hindu Trinity.

Viśōbā Khēcar Saint from Mahārāṣṭra and Guru of Nāmadēv.

Vṛndāvan Town in Mathura, India, where Lord Kṛṣṇa spent His childhood.

Vyāsa Father of Śuka, compiler of the Vēdas, and author of the *Purāṇas, Brahmasūtras, Mahābhārata* and the *Śrīmad Bhāgavatam.*

yajña Vēdic ritual performed before a sacred fire.

Yama Lord of Death.

Yaśodā Foster mother of Kṛṣṇa.

yōga From '*yuj*' (*samādhau*), which means 'to concentrate the mind;' '*yuj*' (*samyamanē*), which means 'to control;' and '*yujir*' (*yōgē*), which means 'to unite.' Union with the Supreme Being. A broad term, it also refers to the various methods of practices through which one can attain oneness with the Divine. A path that leads to Self-realization.

yuga According to Hindu cosmogony, the universe (from origin to dissolution) passes through a cycle made up of four Yugas or ages. The first is Kṛta Yuga (also known as Satya Yuga), during which dharma reigns in society. Each succeeding age sees the progressive decline of dharma. The second age is known as Trētā Yuga, the third is Dvāpara Yuga, and the fourth and present epoch is known as Kali Yuga.

About the Author

Swāmi Amṛtagītānanda Puri is one of Amma's senior monastic disciples. He joined the āśram in 1986 and received initiation into sanyās in 1994. Swāmi is well-versed in Hindu scriptures and is one of the *ācāryas* (scriptural teachers) in Amṛtapuri. Some of the most popular bhajans from the āśram have been written and scored by him. At present, he is the sanyāsī-in-charge of Amma's āśram in Bangalore.

www.ingramcontent.com/pod-product-compliance
Lightning Source LLC
Chambersburg PA
CBHW071211090426
42736CB00014B/2780
* 9 7 8 1 6 8 0 3 7 7 0 7 1 *